Cynthia has been doing DEI work from the very beginning. There are few as expert or thoughtful when it comes to making it work at a company. This book shares her pragmatic advice on how to think about and—more importantly—do it, especially if you're not an HR practitioner.

—**MARTINA LAUCHENGCO,** Partner at Costanoa Ventures

Creating an organizational culture that is diverse, equitable, and inclusive is the most difficult people-related problem businesses face today. *All Are Welcome* brings an innovative, practical, data-driven, step-by-step approach that can help any business leader navigate their journey into this work.

—**RICH JACQUET,** SVP and Chief People Officer of Coursera

Cynthia is an experienced DEIB leader who accelerates change and inclusion in the organizations she joins. I'm lucky to have seen her in action and learned from her. Her book captures a career's worth of experience and learnings into a blueprint that can help us all do better at moving toward a more diverse and inclusive workplace.

—**TOBIN MCDANIEL,** General Manager of SoFi Invest and former Chief of Staff to Charles R. Schwab

In *All Are Welcome*, Cynthia Owyoung offers practical definitions, examples, and actions you can use to align DEIB strategies to your company's values, culture, and business priorities. Cynthia brings deep passion for her work in DEIB together with extensive experience across industries to bring you thoughtful guidance that will help you accelerate the progress of this critical work through your organization. Start turning the pages to build your playbook and take action!

—**ELIZABETH KING,** General Partner and Head of Talent at Edward Jones

This book is packed with actionable insights and tools that will guide DEIB implementation at any level of the organization. It makes a strong argument that DEIB is the whole organization's responsibility, not just HR's. Whether you are new to DEIB work or an old pro, this book has something for you.

—**MATT GILL,** Global Head of Diversity, Equity, Inclusion, and Belonging at Allbirds

*All Are Welcome* is a must-read for anyone looking to create a step change in diversity and inclusion at their organization and reach a broader, more diverse customer base. Cynthia Owyoung serves up fresh insights and the practical tools every leader needs to accelerate lasting change.

—**MARIE CHANDOHA,** retired CEO of Charles Schwab Investment Management

So much activity in the D&I space can be summarized as "diversity theater": going through the motions to give the appearance of caring about diversity without making an actual impact. Cynthia Owyoung's *All Are Welcome* is a valuable guide on how to drive change in diversity, equity, inclusion, and belonging. This book will help you avoid the pitfalls of diversity theater so you can deliver tangible business results for your company and economic and social justice for society.

—**HUGH MOLOTSI,** CEO of Ujama and author of *The Intrapreneur's Journey*

*All Are Welcome* is a business book first, which is what distinguishes it in this field. If you are a business leader challenged by the complexity and sensitivity of diversity and inclusion issues, read this book. You will learn how to create a culture of inclusion that leads to high-performance business results. You will get the data, examples, tools, and practical actions you can take to build an organization that attracts, grows, and retains diverse employees from entry to executive level. It's a must-read to compete for great talent in the coming decade.

—**Susan Burnett,** CEO of Designing Your Life Consulting
and former Chief Learning Officer of Deloitte

The future of work and the workforce is changing. It's no longer sufficient to just talk about how important diversity, equity, inclusion, and belonging (DEIB) are, but now more than ever, it is critical for companies to do something about it. Cynthia gives you wonderful frameworks and strategies on how to practically apply them in your workplace.

—**Ginny Lee,** former President and COO of Khan
Academy and former SVP/GM of Intuit

There are thousands of books written about DEIB, but if you want authenticity paired with passion, you must read *All Are Welcome*. This book is easy to read, practical, and can be put to use immediately. For Cynthia, DEIB is not just a job and this is not just another book; this is her life's mission.

—**Stacey Stevenson,** CEO of Family Equality

Cynthia Owyoung has written an indispensable primer for anyone who wants to understand the critical business reasons for organizations to examine their diversity and inclusion imperatives. Advancing workplace opportunities to embrace diversity is more important today than ever before. Consumers are taking their business to companies with a successful commitment to diversity. Employees are looking to leadership to make a positive difference. Cynthia facilitates the path to DEIB.

—**TERRI KALLSEN,** COO of Wealth Enhancement Group

Cynthia strikes a perfect and much-needed balance between being an I&D heavy hitter, leading initiatives at major companies, and being a relatable and genuine person you would want as a friend. This book is a must-have for a more dynamic, harmonious, and productive workplace.

—**DION LIM,** anchor and reporter for ABC7 News
Bay Area and author of *Make Your Moment*

*All Are Welcome* is easily one of the most comprehensive looks at how to examine an organization's diversity, equity, and inclusion practices and to transform it to drive true business impact.

—**REGINA WALLACE-JONES,** SVP of Product and Engineering
at Mindbody and Mayor of East Palo Alto

Cynthia is a world-class DEIB expert. Make no mistake, this is the corporate handbook for serious executives wanting to take DEIB action, measure it, and align it with current and future company goals. Cynthia's magic is in taking leaders through the change that is necessary for DEIB actions to have measurable results and ultimately impact the bottom line.

—**ELAINE MARINO,** Global Head of Diversity,
Equity, and Inclusion at CrossFit

I had the great good fortune to work directly with Cynthia and see her approach in action. She made a significant, practical difference to workplace culture, to understanding of and commitment to DEI across the organization, and to workforce engagement. Cynthia has outstanding strategic skills and the ability to convert her strategy to implement meaningful change. This book will help you replicate Cynthia's success and impact so that you too can make a measurable difference in all aspects of DEI.

—**ELAINE LOGUE,** retired SVP of First Line Risk
Management at Charles Schwab

# ALL ARE WELCOME

## HOW TO BUILD A REAL WORKPLACE CULTURE OF INCLUSION THAT DELIVERS RESULTS

## CYNTHIA OWYOUNG

NEW YORK   CHICAGO   SAN FRANCISCO   ATHENS   LONDON
MADRID   MEXICO CITY   MILAN   NEW DELHI
SINGAPORE   SYDNEY   TORONTO

1 2 3 4 5 6 7 8 9   LCR   26 25 24 23 22 21

ISBN   978-1-264-26978-5
MHID      1-264-26978-1

e-ISBN  978-1-264-26979-2
e-MHID     1-264-26979-X

Design by Mauna Eichner and Lee Fukui

McGraw Hill books are available at special quantity discounts to use as premiums and sales promotions or for use in corporate training programs. To contact a representative, please visit the Contact Us pages at www.mhprofessional.com.

McGraw Hill is committed to making our products accessible to all learners. To learn more about the available support and accommodations we offer, please contact us at accessibility@mheducation.com. We also participate in the Access Text Network (www.accesstext.org), and ATN members may submit requests through ATN.

*To everyone doing the hard work—*
*keep going*

# Contents

# Acknowledgments

As an Asian woman in the diversity, equity, inclusion, and belonging (DEIB) field, I am very cognizant of the fact that I am relatively rare. Because of the model minority myth in which Asians are perceived as smart and successful, Asians are often not included in the diversity conversation. The obvious underrepresentation of women and other racial or ethnic minorities like Black, Latinx, and Indigenous peoples has rightfully garnered more focus. But this has meant that the disproportionately low representation of Asians in leadership roles, particularly in tech, does not get much scrutiny as a result.

Which is one of the reasons why I feel it's important for me to do DEIB work. You can't ignore the fact that I'm Asian when I'm talking about DEIB. Asians are part of the DEIB conversation whether you think they should be or not. And we must stand in solidarity with all marginalized communities to demand and drive more progress where our diversity is needed.

To be where I am today, writing this book, took a lot of people believing in me and my dedication to making a positive difference in the world. This book is the culmination of not only the experiences I've had but also of the trust that so many people have placed in me to have their backs, represent their voices, and fight the good fights on their behalf in rooms and at tables where they were not invited.

Thank you to everyone I've worked with through the years for all that you've taught me about the power of our humanity. To all my fellow DEIB colleagues who are putting in the hard work day in and day out, you inspire me, and I learn from all of you every day. I am especially grateful to a few folks I have to mention by name for the incredible impact they've made in my life. They have shaped who I am, how I lead, and what this book is about.

Thank you to my initial editor, Amy Li, who first reached out and asked me if I might want to write a book. I appreciate your faith in me to get something worthwhile out of my brain and onto the proverbial page. Thank you to all the folks at McGraw Hill for supporting this book's evolution and debut to the rest of the world. Big thanks to my friend Humberto Tam, whose graphic design skills helped bring some of these concepts to life.

Thank you also to the many dear friends and colleagues whose work, experiences and insights inspired different aspects of this book, including Aubrey Blanche, Susan Cooney, Michelle MiJung Kim, Jonathan Mayes, Johnathan Meade, Leslie Orellana, Olivia Shen Green, Mai Ton, Jessie Wusthoff, and every person who has worked on my past teams. Your wisdom and perspectives are so appreciated and will enlighten others to the many different paths they can take to drive DEIB.

I also have to thank the people who have shaped and supported my DEIB career and leadership over the years: Eduardo Salaz, Jim Grenier, Sherry Whiteley, Loree Farrar, Stacy Parson, Susan Burnett, Rich Jacquet, Becky Cantieri, Dean Chabrier, David Windley, Jennifer Betti, Carin Taylor, Elizabeth King, and Rob Mundell. Your guidance and support may have seemed inconsequential to you at the time but they meant so much more to me and continue to affect me today.

Lastly and most importantly, thank you to my family. Mom, Dad, Bruce, and Arthur, you all have shaped me in profound ways to be the person I am today. I hope I make you proud. To my husband, Barry Fong, and my two kids, Grayson and Bennett, thank you for all your sacrifices to help me make the world a better place. I cannot put into words how much you all mean to me. I couldn't do what I do without you.

# Introduction

Before we talk about anything related to diversity, equity, inclusion, or belonging (DEIB), we have to talk about why I do this work, which is integral to why I'm writing this book. Like many people who are involved in advocating for DEIB, this is deeply personal for me. What makes it personal, you ask? Let's start with how I define who I am.

I am an Asian woman. I'm also a first-generation daughter of immigrants from China who came to the United States with very little money and only the promise of the American dream. I have two brothers. One of them is gay. The other is developmentally disabled. I grew up in a lower-middle-class neighborhood, where the majority of my neighbors were Black. My father served in the Air Force before working his way through community college to become a civil engineer for the city of San Francisco. My mother worked as a seamstress for most of her life, doing piecework at home when I was in elementary school, so she could still take care of us kids. She ultimately transitioned to working full-time in a sewing factory, where she stayed for most of her working life. I am heterosexual, married to a wonderful husband, with whom I have two kids. My husband and I both grew up in the Buddhist tradition, and although our kids now go to Catholic school, we consider ourselves atheists.

Growing up, I experienced discrimination, harassment, and bias through many different lenses. I saw how my parents struggled with my brother's developmental challenges within a cultural context where disabilities were seen as a source of shame for the family and talking about it was taboo. In one of my most distinct childhood memories, I was maybe 10 years old and sitting at the dining table one night for family dinner. My brother accidentally spilled his cup of milk on the table. My dad immediately yelled at him in Chinese for being stupid and clumsy. My brother's face expressed the worthlessness he felt in that moment. I remember thinking, "He doesn't deserve to be yelled at like that. It's just spilled milk." Then it dawned on me that my father saw it as an indicator of my brother's disability, which led to the overreaction. Witnessing how unfairly my brother was treated because of his disability left an indelible imprint on my heart. This was the seed that led me to pursue a career in DEI and the reason I'm writing this book.

Similarly, when my other brother came out as gay to my parents, they couldn't accept it. Thankfully, they didn't disown him or throw him out of the house, as many parents have done with their LGBTQ+ children, but they did tell him not to tell anybody else in the family or flaunt it in any way. They did not want to meet any boyfriend of his or see any gay pride flags flying on his car or at his apartment.

My brother was disappointed in their reaction, but, honestly, it wasn't a surprise. Because many people at the time—and still, to some degree, today—considered being LGBTQ+ "unnatural," I was just glad that my brother was brave enough to embrace who he is and express it, even if others were not receptive. But what cuts deepest is what he had to go through to get to that place of empowerment: depression, isolation, years of putting energy into a façade that never seemed right on him. It was a difficult road. I watched him suffer, and I didn't like it. No one should be told who they can and cannot love. And this strong belief underlines why I am motivated to encourage environments of acceptance and inclusion for anyone who might be different from the majority norm.

As for myself, I've never felt like I really fit in anywhere. For much of my childhood, I was the odd one out. I was never Chinese enough for my Chinese-speaking friends, and I was definitely not American enough (translation: white) to feel like I fit into American culture. I studied hard at school, but my introverted nature meant that I wasn't part of the popular crowd. I tried to fit into the Black cliques at school, but I was clearly not one of them either.

So where did I fit in? I don't think I really found my community until I was in high school, where I ended up making friends with people who also walked a more multicultural path, either as immigrants themselves or American-born Chinese (ABCs), like me. I've always felt like I had to carve out my own path as a result, and that perhaps has led to a need to create more connection and a sense of belonging for others.

But I've also seen the power of diversity. In middle school, I played in the orchestra. It was probably one of the most diverse orchestras you will ever see, with Black, Latinx, Asian, and white people playing violins, violas, cellos, bass, and piano, all (mostly) in harmony with each other. It didn't matter if you didn't speak English well, as long as you could read music. It didn't matter if you weren't getting straight As in class, as long as you showed up for practice. It didn't matter if you didn't have money to afford instruments since we were all borrowing our instruments from the school. We were taught that music doesn't just come out of the instrument you play. It comes from how you play it, and each of us brought our own special soul to how we played.

When we all came together around a piece of music, each playing our different parts and each playing off one another, we created a symphony. I took that experience to heart as a very real and tangible example of how diversity can come together to create something bigger than each individual. The different parts really do make something bigger than the whole.

These are just a few examples of many formative experiences that motivated me to become a DEIB professional.

Over the years, I've had the good fortune to work at some great companies that have been fully committed to making progress in this space. I was part of the founding diversity and inclusion team at Intuit, where I helped develop and launch their first corporate diversity strategy with companywide training and employee resource groups, supported by a robust executive diversity council.

Then I got the opportunity to do similar things and more on a global scale at Yahoo!, where I was able to expand my scope to include employee engagement programs, talent management, and organizational development work. From there, I led talent development and internal inclusion initiatives at a hypergrowth startup, before leaving to launch my own consulting practice focused on leadership development for women of color and inclusion strategies for companies. I contracted with companies of all sizes, from biotech to consumer services, helping their DEIB, human resources, and leadership teams develop and implement DEIB strategies.

After that, I decided to step outside of my comfort zone and enter financial services for the chance to make a difference in an industry that has such a profound impact on economic opportunity. I firmly believe that you cannot have social justice without economic justice as well, so addressing DEIB in financial services has the potential to drive a more equitable society through wealth building in communities that have historically been shut out and left behind. It's a lofty goal that will take more than my lifetime to achieve, but I'm determined to do my part to get us that much closer.

## WHO SHOULD READ THIS BOOK?

While I have been doing this work from within an HR department for all of my career, DEIB is not a uniquely HR function. This playbook is really for any leader of an organization that wants to drive change. In fact, if you are leading a business line or function outside of HR, I really appreciate that you're reading this book because ultimately, you are the person who will make the key decisions necessary to determine whether progress will be made.

DEIB work is everyone's responsibility, from the frontline worker to the CEO. It will be a journey, and you won't always get things right. As long as I've been doing this work, I've put my foot in my mouth on a regular basis. The field of DEIB is constantly evolving, and what works for one will not work for all. What works today won't necessarily work tomorrow. And what works for your company won't always work at other companies.

Context matters, and it's constantly shifting. Get used to feeling like you don't know everything because you don't. But if you're persistent, open to experimentation, and willing to admit what you don't know, you just might lead the way for others to follow in driving DEIB for all.

## HOW TO READ THIS BOOK

Being a DEIB practitioner is a hard job. It often feels like you are pushing a rock uphill, and after a while, if you're not able to push that rock up far enough or fast enough, it might feel like it's time to find something else to do before the rock starts rolling back toward you. Many have asked me how I've stayed in this space as long as I have. I tell them I'm extremely stubborn. I won't quit until I've reached my goal of accelerating progress in DEIB across a large swath of corporate America. And that is why this book is important. It's my way of imparting to anyone willing to read it all the lessons I've learned doing DEIB work for the past 20 years in companies big and small, across different industries, and within different cultures and conditions for success.

This is your playbook for how to approach DEIB work in a way that will support real progress in your companies, if you're truly willing to do what it takes. Keep in mind that I'm not here to give you general platitudes like "hire more Black people" or provide you with a list of things to check off like unconscious bias training so you can show others that you're doing something. In my experience, that isn't particularly helpful.

My intention is to share the behind-the-scenes actions you need to consider as you actually implement a thoughtful approach to DEIB and to give you a road map of pitfalls to avoid and ways to think about this work that go deeper than surface level. In an effort to protect confidentiality, I've masked identities, changed details, or created a composite of several situations I've encountered in some of the stories shared. My goal is to help you successfully navigate the inherent tension between prioritizing the business and prioritizing DEIB, because they don't have to always be at odds with each other.

If your goal is to develop a real culture of inclusion that will result in more dimensions of diversity represented at all levels of your organization, highly engaged employees of all backgrounds being productive and thriving, and a business that is innovative and leading the marketplace, then applying this playbook will help you get there.

Please remember that this book is not a step-by-step instruction guide specific to your company or geography. Rather, it is a more general road map with guiding principles that you can apply to any situation and modify according to your needs. For example, I'll refer to "race and ethnicity," which has a very specific context in the United States, but it will mean something different in other countries around the world.

In your organization, the dimensions of diversity that are important to focus on will vary depending on your demographics, your culture, and your industry, among other factors. It's important to assess your company needs within the broader context it operates in and develop a set of strategies and a road map that is most relevant to you. Within each chapter, I've included exercises to bring these concepts to life and help you begin doing the real work needed to start making progress building a high-performing workplace culture of diversity, equity, inclusion, and belonging.

Let's get started.

## CHAPTER 1

# Defining Diversity, Equity, Inclusion, and Belonging (DEIB): The What, Why, and How

When I go to an industry networking event or informal social gathering, I often get asked about what I do for a living, as I'm sure many of us are. When I tell people that I help companies improve their diversity and inclusion, I usually get the follow-up question of, "What is that about?" So it's worth starting off with the basics of what we mean when we talk about diversity, equity, inclusion, and belonging, why it's important, and how to diagnose where your issues are. We'll dive into each of these areas in this chapter.

## WHAT BASIC TERMS YOU NEED TO KNOW

The world of diversity, equity, inclusion, and belonging has evolved quite a bit over the years. When I first started looking into careers in this space back in 2000, only large companies had internal personnel dedicated to diversity and inclusion work. At the time, IBM, Sodexo, Charles Schwab, and Genentech were some examples of companies across different industries that had over 10,000 employees and executives directly responsible for creating more diverse and inclusive workplaces, but they were more exceptions to the rule than the rule itself. I remember searching on the internet for jobs with "diversity" in the title and coming up with only a handful of positions. Back then, most diversity-oriented roles were seen as compliance based—meaning that companies had to dedicate resources to closing demographic representation gaps because of government regulations to do so. This resulted in many diversity roles being coupled with affirmative action responsibilities, which brings us to our first term to define.

According to the *Encyclopaedia Britannica*, "*Affirmative action*, in the United States, is an active effort to improve employment or educational opportunities for members of minority groups and for women."[1] There are only four dimensions of diversity—gender, race and/or ethnicity, disability, and military status—that firms are legally obligated to measure in the United States through self-identification forms. Within corporations, affirmative action is often misinterpreted as requiring quotas for hiring people based on these demographic characteristics, without regard to whether they are the most qualified people for the job or not.

This interpretation has formed the most common argument against diversity efforts, which is that in a meritocracy, only your abilities should determine whether you are selected for a role or able to advance inside a company. Your demographic background shouldn't matter. It's all about objective qualifications. However, both viewpoints are flawed because affirmative action isn't about hiring quotas, and true meritocracies don't exist. What affirmative action actually means in practice is that companies required by law to adhere to this policy must make good faith efforts to attain representation parity between their workforce and whatever the available, qualified talent pools are within the geographical area from which they recruit for each job category within the company. *Good faith efforts* essentially means that companies have to take actions to try to close any representation gaps that might exist. It does *not* mean that they have to hire people based only on their race or gender.

Affirmative action and diversity are two separate and distinct concepts. While many companies engage in affirmative action as a matter of compliance with US federal laws, it is not the same thing as driving diversity in the workplace. While affirmative action and diversity are both about representation, affirmative action is more limited in its scope. The rules that US federal government contractors must adhere to in support of affirmative action are designed to span across all industries, and therefore the rules meet the lowest common denominator. In other words, while affirmative action analyses and plans can be incredibly useful inputs to diversity strategies and efforts, they go only so far, and they must be supplemented by other activities that go beyond limited representation.

*Diversity* in the context of a workplace really means bringing people who are different from each other—with their own unique characteristics, backgrounds, experiences, and perspectives—together to realize the strengths of those differences. It encompasses much more than just race and gender, which are often the focus of affirmative action, and it demands that people think more broadly about the various dimensions of diversity that can be leveraged for success. The model shown in Figure 1.1 is one that I've often referenced in my work and found particularly helpful. It was created by Lee Gardenswartz and Anita Rowe, who have been pioneers in diversity education since 1977.[2]

The model describes the Five Layers of Global Diversity, using concentric circles to illustrate how we are all made up of various dimensions of diversity. Your Personality is at the core, followed by a ring of Internal Dimensions as defined by your demographics, like race, age, and gender. The next circle shows the External Dimensions that shape

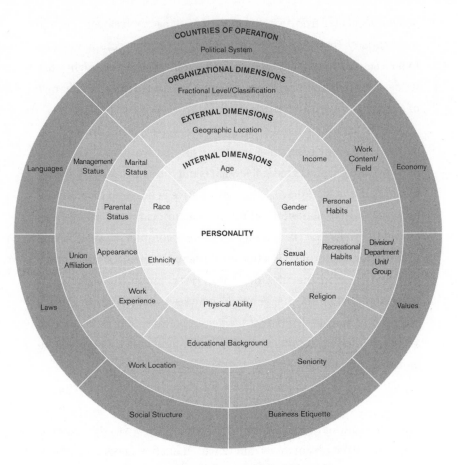

Figure 1.1 **Five Layers of Global Diversity**

*Source:* Republished with permission and adapted from Lee Gardenswartz and Anita Rowe, *Diverse Teams at Work*, Second Edition (Alexandria, VA: SHRM, 2003); and Lee Gardenswartz, Anita Rowe, Patricia Digh, and Martin Bennett, *The Global Diversity Desk Reference* (San Francisco: Pfeiffer, 2003). Internal Dimensions and External Dimensions are adapted from Marilyn Loden and Judy Rosener, *Workplace America!* (Homewood, IL: Business One Irwin, 1991). © 2010 by Lee Gardenswartz and Anita Rowe. All rights reserved. Permission conveyed through Copyright Clearance Center, Inc.

who you are, like education and income. The circle after that shows the Organizational Dimensions, which encompass characteristics typically used to define yourself at work, like job level or work location. Finally, the outermost circle—Countries of Operation—consists of dimensions defining the cultures in which you operate, including language, laws, and values that affect your cultural viewpoint. Each person has a unique perspective that is informed by each of these layers.

Growing up in the United States, I have a very different lens on DEIB than I would have if I had grown up in China, as my parents did. Having a marketing background means I do not look at employee issues in the same way as my colleagues who have been in only human resources. And being able-bodied means I don't experience accessibility issues to physical environments in the way that people with mobility issues do. There are many characteristics we use to define our identities, and it's important to recognize that each person has both visible and invisible identities that we may not be aware of. Being cognizant of how different contexts inform different perspectives is incredibly important to developing an appropriate action plan that is inclusive of and relevant to different issues.

You often see *diversity* and *inclusion* used together in a phrase, and indeed, the two concepts go together, but they are not interchangeable. *Diversity* refers to representation across characteristics that make people who they are, and *inclusion* actually means ensuring that no one is held back from full participation within the organization. Inclusion strives to leverage diversity within the organization to its fullest potential.

An analogy I love that delineates really succinctly the difference between diversity and inclusion was coined by Vernā Myers, the current VP of inclusion strategy at Netflix: "Diversity is being invited to the party. Inclusion is being asked to dance."[3] I remember how important it was for me to be asked to dance when I was considering whether to take an executive diversity and inclusion (D&I) role. I realized that I would be the only person of color at that level in human resources at the company. And while I was not reporting directly to the chief human resources officer (CHRO), I would still be a member of the HR leadership team responsible for making HR policy and program decisions affecting the company.

That I would be on the HR leadership team was a key reason why I decided to take the role. Not only did the company give me a leadership seat at the table, but I felt strongly included during meetings, where I could fully participate and have my perspective taken seriously. This is a very real example of why having diversity is not enough. It must also be coupled with inclusion to reap the benefits of what that diversity brings to your organization. It's relatively easy to bring diversity into an organization. It's much harder to create a truly inclusive culture in which that diversity wants to stay.

## When Did Equity (*E*) and Belonging (*B*) Join?

For many decades, the field focused only on diversity and inclusion. But in recent years, companies have started to add in some newer terms to ensure that diversity goes beyond just checking off that box.

Equity is the key outcome of driving for more diversity and inclusion within an organization. Equity is often confused with equality because they both seek the same outcome—fair treatment for everyone. However, where *equality* is about everyone getting the same opportunities, access, and resources, *equity* acknowledges that not everyone needs the same things to succeed. Equity is about giving people what they need.

At one company, they made a concerted effort to hire people who came from nontraditional industry backgrounds into entry-level customer service roles. Historically, they had tended to favor people with prior experience in that industry. However, what they found was that the people who ultimately succeeded the most in these roles weren't people who had prior knowledge or experience. Rather, it was the people who really enjoyed building relationships with customers and helping them.

But after hiring these folks, it became clear that they were not passing the required training certifications—another important step in their success—at the same rates as those with backgrounds in the industry. This was negatively affecting their ability to retain more underrepresented groups including women and ethnic minorities, who made up a bigger proportion of those without prior industry experience. Consequently, they set out to redesign their training process to allow for different time frames and types of support, like mentoring, aligned to people at different levels of industry knowledge and experience. This resulted in more consistent pass rates across different demographics. This was equity in action: giving people different resources based on their individual circumstances and needs. The cartoon in Figure 1.2 really illustrates this difference.

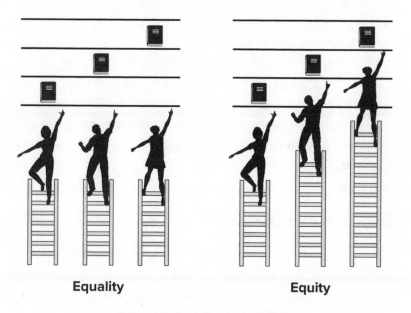

**Equality**                    **Equity**

Figure 1.2 **Equality Versus Equity**

A more recent concept to be connected to diversity and inclusion in the workplace is the idea of belonging. *Belonging* is the sense of connection one has to a group. Do I feel like I fit in? Am I considered a valued member of the team? Will they accept me for who I am? Belonging is highly related to inclusion in that you can't have belonging without inclusion. It's one thing to be welcomed initially into a group. It's quite another thing to feel like this is a group you are comfortable staying in for the long term.

The longest job I ever stayed in was at Yahoo!. It was a place where I felt a strong sense of belonging, where employees were united in the sense of being underdogs in the tech industry, trying to survive in a Google-dominated world. Employees at Yahoo! described themselves as "bleeding purple," the company's brand color, to signify how strongly they connected to the company and its mission. In addition to that, I had the rare experience of serving under two female CEOs at the tech company, and there were many Asians in leadership roles throughout my tenure, which signaled that significant barriers for people like me to climb the corporate ladder did not exist.

The company's culture and values really spoke to me, and I appreciated feeling like I wasn't limited in what I could achieve there. My sense of belonging to the company was so strong that even now, more than five years since leaving the company, I still tell people that I bleed purple and will never give up my Yahoo! email account. That's the power of belonging.

## Other Important Concepts

Another term that's important to talk about is *underrepresented groups* (URGs), an umbrella term used historically to refer to *marginalized communities*, including women, people of color, people with disabilities, LGBTQ+ people, and anyone else who isn't fully represented in the workplace. You'll notice I use this term extensively instead of *minorities* because it is much broader than just race or ethnicity, which is typically what *minorities* refers to.

I also encourage you to stay away from referring to underrepresented groups as "diverse communities." Every community is diverse based on the definition of *diversity* I gave earlier. Rather than using *diverse communities* as a way of avoiding saying Black or Brown people, or any other dimension that makes you feel uncomfortable being specific about, it's preferable to speak directly to the issues we are trying to solve for, which at their core are underrepresentation and inequitable treatment. Many companies define their efforts even more specifically around BIPOC (which stands for Black, Indigenous, and people of color) communities in an effort to center their needs.

Lastly, we can't talk about underrepresentation and inequitable treatment without also talking about bias. *Bias* is defined as a tendency or inclination in favor of or against an idea or thing, usually in a way that is perceived as unfair. We all have biases, both conscious and unconscious. These are sometimes referred to as *explicit* versus *implicit*, respectively, where *explicit* refers to biases that we express intentionally, and *implicit* refers to biases that we are not necessarily fully aware of and that are often unintentional. Some biases are good, like choosing to eat healthy food, and some biases are not so good, like assuming an older person can't use technology.

Having biases doesn't make anyone a bad person. In fact, biases are part of being human and are largely helpful to us in that they are cognitive shortcuts that allow us to make quicker sense of the world. We just need to be careful about ensuring that our biases don't lead to inaccurate or unreasonable conclusions about people. It is one of the underlying reasons why some people are more advantaged or disadvantaged than others. We tend to feel more positive toward people we perceive to be more like ourselves and ascribe more positive traits to people we are comfortable and familiar with. It's important to raise our awareness of the different types of biases we have and take steps to mitigate or counteract potential negative impacts from them where possible.

There are a ton of other DEIB-related terms that would take more than one book to explain, but if you're serious about DEIB work, get to know terms like *cisgender, cultural appropriation*, and *intersectionality*, among others. I recommend starting with the Harvard Office for Diversity, Inclusion & Belonging's *DIB Glossary: Foundational Concepts & Affirming Language* and branching out from there.[4] Do your research online, and look for reputable and varied sources.

One of the questions I am asked most often is, "What are the most appropriate terms to use when referring to [insert diversity characteristic here]?" I recognize that diversity-related terminology can sometimes feel like a minefield. No one wants to offend people inadvertently, and it's easy to do when you're not well versed in the right language. But it's important to understand that language is an ever-evolving construct and what is acceptable terminology today might not be 10 years from now.

Take the word *handicapped* to describe a person with a disability, for example. A few decades ago, this was the acceptable term. However, as more people equated the meaning of *handicapped* as tied to begging on the streets with "cap in hand," it became offensive to use the term when describing a person with a disability. As a general rule of thumb, it's much more acceptable to use *person-first terminology*, with which you recognize the person first, then the disability. So instead of saying, "a blind person," you would say, "a person who is blind."

It's also important to note that what one person finds acceptable another may not. Some people identify as a person with a disability, but others prefer to identify as differently abled. Some people identify as Black, and others prefer to be referred to as African American. It's really not about getting terminology "right" all the time but, instead, about using the most broadly acceptable terms when referring to a group, and making the effort to ask individuals how they would prefer to be identified when you are interacting with them. It can be really helpful to read first-person accounts of why someone prefers one term over another. Keep in mind that what works in one context might be received differently in another, but don't let that stop you from getting started on your own journey of discovery.

## PUTTING IT INTO ACTION

- Think about a time when you felt excluded in your life. How did it make you feel? Come up with a word or short phrase to describe the emotion that most dominates that memory.

- Ask a few of your friends to do the same exercise and share their emotion words with you. Do you see any commonalities among the words shared?

- I've asked this question of various individuals and groups dozens of times throughout the years, and I've seen many of the same words come up over and over again—*frustration*, *embarrassment*, *sadness*, *isolation*, *anger*, *loneliness*, and so on (Figure 1.3). If you or people on your team were coming into work every day feeling any of these emotions, do you think they would be very productive? I don't think they would be.

anger defeated marginalized
helpless unworthy irrelevant
left targeted lonely ostracized
isolated upset embarrassed
unwanted alone betrayed
angry sad hurt resilient
bad outsider
confused guilty disappointed mad hurt
despondent different disrespected sadness
shame belittled worthless

Figure 1.3 **Word Cloud for Feelings of Exclusion**

- Is it fair to expect people feeling this way to be performing at their best? No, it's not, but that is what we ask people to do when we don't address the latest harassment or discrimination headline in our workplaces.

- Do situations of exclusion happen only to people in underrepresented groups? I think you would be hard-pressed to find anyone who hasn't experienced a single time in their lives where they felt excluded.

- This is why DEIB work is so relevant to everyone in every workplace. It's not just an underrepresented group problem to solve. It's everyone's problem to solve.

## WHY IS DEIB IMPORTANT?

I mentioned earlier that relatively few companies were hiring for DEIB roles 20 years ago. For someone who was trying to break into the field with no professional background in HR, at a time when the first dot-com bubble had just burst, causing havoc in the marketplace and kicking off a recession that was then exacerbated by the events of September 11, 2001, it is a bit of an understatement to say that it was a challenge to make the transition to a DEIB career. These kinds of roles were few and far between, and it took me two years of contracting, networking, and volunteering to finally land that elusive full-time diversity role at a tech company within commuting distance of my home.

Contrast that with today, when a search for "inclusion and diversity" job titles on Indeed.com yields 84 jobs available in the San Francisco Bay Area.[5] Companies as small as 100 people now have diversity committees, and it seems any company doing any significant volume in hiring either already has or is currently looking for at least one diversity role in-house. According to LinkedIn, the number of diversity roles at organizations grew by 71 percent in just five years, from 2015 to 2020.[6] This is good news. Over the years, company leaders have woken up to the fact that they need to focus on DEIB. Maybe you're one of them, since you've decided to read this book. Or maybe you're just curious about the topic and haven't yet thought about why DEIB should be important to your company. Whatever your starting point, you need to understand the business case for diversity and develop one for your own organization to motivate stronger engagement and progress.

First things first, let's establish right off the bat that doing DEIB work is the morally right thing to do. If we believe everyone has the same basic human rights, then equal access to opportunities for everyone and the basic right to respect and dignity should be a no-brainer. Therefore, every company should be striving for equal representation in their ranks and an inclusive environment for all to thrive and belong. But every company isn't actually doing that so we know that moral arguments only go so far. While fundamentally, I think business cases for DEIB shouldn't be necessary and are used more often as excuses for inaction, I also believe we should treat DEIB initiatives just like any other business initiative within a company, and that means developing a business case to justify resourcing against it.

Developing a business case means answering a few simple questions:

1. What problem am I trying to solve?
2. What are the benefits of solving it?
3. What resources will be needed to solve it?

## What Am I Solving For?

Let's start with defining the problem. First, create a macro view of the business problem. It doesn't take much effort to find some sobering statistics on the state of diversity in business from either a local or global lens. You should also research diversity statistics specific to your industry through government sources, academic and nongovernmental organizations, and/or professional organizations. Here is just a sampling of studies that highlight the gaps in representation of various dimensions of diversity across the business landscape:

- From 2000 to 2020, there was little increase in the Fortune 500's CEO diversity. White men held 96.4 percent of the Fortune 500 CEO positions in 2000, and they still held 85.8 percent in 2020. Only 1 percent of the Fortune 500 CEOs in 2020 were African Americans, only 2.4 percent were East Asians or South Asians, and only 3.4 percent were Latinx.[7]

- Women accounted for less than a third (29 percent) of senior roles globally in 2019.[8]

- Across 34 countries surveyed by the Pew Research Center in 2019, a median of 52 percent agreed that homosexuality should be accepted with 38 percent saying that it should be discouraged.[9]

- In developing countries according to the United Nations as recently as 2021, 80 to 90 percent of persons with disabilities of working age were unemployed, whereas in industrialized countries, the figure was between 50 and 70 percent.[10]

- In the United States, Black and Hispanic workers have continued to be underrepresented in the STEM workforce. According to Pew Research in 2018, Black people made up 11 percent of the US workforce overall but represented 9 percent of STEM workers, while Hispanic people made up 16 percent of the US workforce but only 7 percent of all STEM workers.[11]

After looking at the overall statistics, you should assess your own organization with a diversity lens to understand any gaps in representation, inclusion experiences, or diverse market needs that may affect your business which need to be addressed. You're really looking for areas where there may be an unintentional disparate impact happening, meaning one group of people is being disproportionately affected by a system, process, or policy that is intended to affect everyone equally.

For example, your hiring process may be unintentionally screening out people who are neurodivergent if it requires taking an exam that means sitting still for two hours, which can be really challenging for someone on the autism spectrum. I worked with a tech company that had a four-hour technical screen that we found was disparately affecting mothers, who were turned off from applying because their family responsibilities deterred them from spending that much time on a technical assignment that might not lead to anything worthwhile.

Your firm may already be collecting information on basic demographics such as age and gender for benefits administration. If your firm is also a federal contractor in the United States, or subject to rules similar to affirmative action in other countries, you may be required to collect race and/or ethnicity information, disability status, and military status. You could also supplement that information with other dimensions of diversity, like sexual orientation, gender identity, national origin, or caretaking status. This can be accomplished through regular surveys to your employees or as part of your onboarding process during hiring.

The key is to focus on dimensions that will be relevant to your DEIB goals. You don't want to measure something for measurement's sake. For example, asking about gender pronouns allows you to address people correctly in emails and during meetings. That is a specific action you can take to help people feel included. However, asking people to identify whether they are bisexual or pansexual isn't likely to be helpful when your actions to support people who identify in either category are not likely to be any different, such as policies prohibiting discrimination and harassment based on sexual orientation.

Probably the most difficult concepts to measure are inclusion and belonging because that is a very personal experience for each individual. The most common indicators for this are employee surveys and attrition rates. In employee surveys, you can ask questions specifically about how strongly people feel they belong inside their teams, or if they feel included in decision-making. Oftentimes, it can be helpful to create or leverage existing diversity climate surveys and inclusion indexes used by many other companies as benchmarks for comparison. Attrition is the natural outcome of employees' not feeling like they belong at a company. There are usually many factors that weigh into a decision to leave a company, but if you can correlate attrition and exit survey results with inclusion and belonging survey items, there is a lot of validity in using attrition as an indicator of inclusion issues that need to be addressed.

Don't discount qualitative feedback from your employees. If you have open feedback channels for employees to submit questions about DEIB, you can gather information about what's on their minds in real time. You can also hold periodic focus groups or attend employee community meetings to hear more about what's going well and what might be challenging. Monitoring the kinds of employee relations issues that come into legal and HR can also give helpful insights as to where there might be concerns that need to be addressed. I always tried to meet with a broad swath of both senior leaders and frontline employees across the company every year to hear about how our DEIB initiatives were going and what we could continue to do better. This was helpful in adding depth and color commentary behind what we were seeing in the engagement and exit survey data.

It's also important to understand how important DEIB is to your clients and other key stakeholders. Is your client base very diverse, and does your employee base reflect that diversity? What are the demographic trends affecting your future business, and are you prepared to meet those future needs? Do DEIB issues matter to your shareholders, lawmakers, and business partners, and are they asking you to demonstrate your commitment? It's important to understand the landscape in which your business operates and ensure that you are proactively addressing DEIB to position the business for future success. When you are working for a large, multinational company that depends on getting as many people to view your content as possible, expanding your marketplace and focusing on DEIB make sense. When you are selling large enterprise software platforms to CIOs, the majority of whom are white males, you may need to find additional reasons to drive DEIB issues.

In cases where reflecting your customer base isn't the most compelling reason to invest in DEIB efforts, don't underestimate the power of standing up for your values as part of your business case. If your company is explicit about DEIB in its values, that is a strong reason to support DEIB initiatives. After all, if you can't stand behind your values with tangible demonstrations of it, then why have values at all? As author and motivational speaker Simon Sinek says, "We are drawn to leaders and organizations that are good at communicating what they believe. Their ability to make us feel like we belong, to make us feel special, safe and not alone is part of what gives them the ability to inspire us."[12] I have found that, particularly in organizations that are built on a foundation of trust and relationships, demonstrating integrity with your value of inclusion is the leading reason to dedicate people and money to DEIB efforts.

## How Will It Affect the Business?

Next, understanding the benefits of focusing on DEIB will show people the upside of putting resources toward these initiatives. What this comes down to is pulling together the key pieces of research that you think will persuade your audience to engage in different actions that they wouldn't engage in otherwise. There is a plethora of research out there with evidence pointing to how diversity and inclusion efforts lead to better business outcomes. To save you some time and effort, because we know both are in short supply these days, here are some key statistics and their sources. I encourage you to read the full studies to get a good grasp of their methodologies and findings:

- McKinsey research shows that gender-diverse companies are 15 percent more likely to outperform their peers and ethnically diverse companies are 35 percent more likely.[13]

- Josh Bersin and Deloitte research found that companies which embrace diversity and inclusion in all aspects of their business statistically outperform their peers. These companies are 1.7 times more likely to be innovation leaders in their market, they have 2.3 times higher cash flow per employee, they have 1.4 times more revenue, and they are 120 percent more capable of meeting financial targets.[14]

- Corporate Executive Board research found that at companies with more diverse and inclusive workforces, employees' discretionary effort was 1.12 times higher and intent to stay was 1.19 times higher.[15]

- *Harvard Business Review* has said that employees at more diverse companies are 45 percent likelier to report that their firm's market share grew over the previous year and 70 percent likelier to report that the firm captured a new market.[16]

If you want more data specific to your industry, you may have to do a deep internet search to uncover it. Or you might think about making an investment for the broader cause and sponsor a research study of your own. This will take some dollars, but for some leaders, it can be the best way to get the information that is most relevant to your company. There are two things I have found to be most helpful in citing external research as part of your company's business case for DEIB: relevancy and recency.

*Relevancy* means citing information that is closely connected to your business. Obviously, if you run a consumer products company, talking about the lack of available women with software development qualifications will not be particularly helpful to your case. But if you're in financial services, talking about how women will control a majority of US wealth by 2030 and comparing that to the lack of women financial advisors in the wealth management industry (just 15 percent) will likely make your leaders pay more attention to the need for DEIB.[17] This is also where partnering with your business development, marketing, or external research departments can be really beneficial to understanding what the business potential of serving more diverse communities is for your company. When you're able to show that the company will make more money by serving a more diverse customer base, then you're able to sway even DEIB skeptics to support DEIB initiatives. I also encourage leaders to think about what communities they are leaving behind when they make business decisions about whom they are serving. It may not change the business decision, but it's important to consider the potential implications and be intentional about it.

*Recency* is necessary because, as we all experience every day, the pace of change is accelerating across the globe and research can get outdated pretty quickly and lose its relevance. Try to find the most recent research or information you can because you don't want your conversation to get derailed by a debate on how old the research you're presenting might be.

At one of my presentations to engineering leaders at a company, the primary feedback I received was that the research I cited was conducted more than five years ago and therefore it was too old to be relevant. This was slightly absurd considering that some of the studies that were originally conducted decades ago have been validated multiple times and in multiple ways since then. But the goal is to eliminate as many barriers to your argument as possible up front, so do your best to anticipate what your audience cares about, and then create a compelling story, both through data and anecdotes, to really illustrate the need.

## Getting Budget and Resources

Once you have a business case for DEIB established, it's necessary to propose the resources needed to solve for the problem you've outlined. It's also important to be cognizant of the broader context of your organization. Meaning, don't ask to go to the moon if your company can barely afford the astronaut suit, let alone the rocket ship you need to get there. It's unrealistic to go to your executive team with a $3 million budget when they just told the entire company to eliminate all nonessential travel expenses for the next year in order to lower your expense ratio.

On the other hand, it's also unrealistic to expect to get anything substantial or meaningful done on a budget of $5 per employee, which was a typical budget I had to work with initially in many companies. As a result of being given such low budgets, I wound up going to individual business leaders to fund different initiatives from their budgets instead, which isn't a great model if you really want to know what your DEIB spend looks like year over year.

What I always find most helpful when asking for resources is to outline three options for leaders to consider. Option A is usually the absolute minimum level of resources you need to make progress against your goals. Option B can be your aspirational ask—that is, the level of resources you'd need to enable you to exceed expectations. Option C should be a middle ground between the two other options. Every option you present should be something you're willing to live with no matter what level of resources you get. And it's important to be clear on what trade-offs will take place as a result of choosing different options.

Your goal is to get to a decision on resourcing and a road map as quickly as possible. It's not to have the most perfect plan in place. It's to get you started because the plan will change over time. I once went to the executive team with a single option, and they asked me to revise it and come back when it was ready. I had to repeat that process about four more times before finally getting their approval. It was not fun, and I learned my lesson after six months of delays: don't get caught in this cycle.

Beware of any company that won't provide you with a significant budget or head count to accomplish your DEIB goals. If this work is truly a company priority, it should be treated like one with appropriate people, responsibilities, and dollars assigned to it. People should not be "volunteering" their time to work on DEIB initiatives. It should be part of their job responsibilities, development plans, performance reviews, and goals for the year, with commensurate compensation tied to their actions and results in this area.

Neither should leaders expect you to increase the diversity represented in your hiring if they won't give you a budget for reaching out to different talent pipelines. You cannot rely on the "post-and-pray method" of hiring, where you post a job and pray that people of diverse backgrounds apply.

Don't blame the lack of diverse job applicants on a lack of diverse talent in the marketplace either. For example, top universities are graduating Black and Hispanic computer scientists and engineers at twice the rate they are being hired by tech companies, busting the myth of the lack of a diverse talent pipeline.[18]

Many people from underrepresented communities also won't bother applying for a role if they haven't seen active outreach by a company to their communities. More and more, underrepresented talent are looking for signals from companies on whether they are truly committed to DEIB. Not having community organization partnerships or sharing information on your DEIB efforts publicly can be a credibility issue.

## PUTTING IT INTO ACTION

- Gather a group of diversity champions together from across your business. Make sure you have all key functions represented, from HR to marketing, and from product development to investor relations.

- Brainstorm reasons why the company needs to focus on DEIB. Follow the rules of brainstorming 101: all ideas get put on the table; there is no judgment. Your goal is to list as many reasons as possible in 20 minutes.

- Review the list, and narrow it down to the most important and impactful reasons. You can do this by giving people a number of votes, say, three, and asking them to put those votes toward the ideas that resonate the most. They can use all three votes on one idea or spread them out. Make sure there is general agreement on the final list before leaving the meeting.

- Ask each member to begin sharing the list with influential leaders in the organization and getting feedback from those leaders. Come back together in two weeks to consolidate and incorporate the feedback as appropriate and finalize the list.

- Do this quickly so that the data you use is up-to-date and relevant before you roll out an action plan.

# HOW TO CONDUCT A DEIB AUDIT

The next step after bringing people on board with DEIB initiatives is to understand your current state to determine where your issues are. It's time to conduct a *DEIB audit*. This means examining all your policies, practices, processes, and systems for issues that may be unintentionally reinforcing current stereotypes or excluding people from different backgrounds. Let's break down a few examples that can provide you with a starting point of ideas for your own audit.

## Examine Your Talent Processes

Hiring practices and policies usually have the best of intentions but often fail to achieve that high bar of hiring only the "best" talent. What most hiring processes actually do is hire only the most available talent who look like most other people at the company.

For example, in hiring, it's common to include an educational or experience requirement in job postings. Depending on the role you are hiring for, this can be highly exclusionary. It's often a shortcut proxy for actually assessing the skill sets that you think experience and education substitute for. I have come across so many hiring managers who want only a graduate from a top-tier school because they came from one themselves. But many great candidates can come from other institutions.

As Leila Janah, a serial entrepreneur and iconic advocate for DEIB who passed away in 2020, said, "Talent is equally distributed, but opportunity is not."[19] Don't ask for a college bachelor's degree if it's not actually needed for the job. There are a lot of amazing technical programmers who never finished high school. I've worked with some of them, so I know they are out there. People like Oprah Winfrey and Bill Gates had not completed their college degrees when they attained huge success. And yet, many companies require college degrees for jobs that don't need them, excluding an entire diverse talent pool from consideration.

Also, if you have a policy that automatically disqualifies everyone with a criminal record, you may be inadvertently excluding many people of color from your talent pool as incarceration rates for Black and Hispanic people are much higher than for white people.[20] Of course, you don't want to hire somebody into an accounting job if they've previously been convicted of embezzlement, but if someone was convicted of shoplifting in their youth more than 10 years ago, you may not want to disqualify them from answering a phone in customer service for a consumer goods company. Many people deserve a chance to leave the stigma of a prison sentence behind, and meaningful employment is one key to doing so.

While it can be difficult to hire people from diverse backgrounds, advancing people from diverse backgrounds inside a company may be even harder to do when you are in a culture that values normative behaviors over nonconformance. It's no secret that leadership is often defined by who is in the majority.[21] There were in fact more CEOs named James in the Fortune 500 in 2018 than there were women.[22]

So it becomes necessary to examine your process for promoting people at your firm to determine whether it is fair and equitable. For example, a typical promotion process I have encountered at companies is basically one that relies on managers' judgment of whether a person on their staff is ready to be promoted. This judgment is often based on some vague and generic job-level criteria that apply across many different job categories at the company. The main deciding factors for promotion in these cases tend to be how long a person has been in the role and whether they have been vocal about getting a promotion. You can see how this would not be equitable to those who may be qualified for the role but perhaps feel uncomfortable asking for a promotion for fear it would be perceived negatively.

A great example of a way to address this problem was used at GoDaddy, a technology firm that overhauled its promotion process not only to evaluate individuals on the basis of specific and consistent criteria related to their impact at the firm but also to consider all employees who were eligible for a promotion at that point in time instead of just those who expressed a desire to be promoted.[23]

Another tactic that has been used successfully by companies like Google is the use of *promotion committees*, which can provide a more objective evaluation of those employees up for promotion. More commonly used in university settings, promotion committees consist of a group of people at senior levels tasked with evaluating the qualifications of candidates for promotions. Members of the promotion committee may or may not have direct experience with the candidates, but they should be able to calibrate across a broad swath of the organization to drive objectivity and consistency in evaluation. This same concept can be applied to hiring as well.

## Review Policies and Practices

In addition to assessing your talent processes for potential bias, it's important to review your policies and systems for ways in which they may either help or hinder your DEIB efforts. Benefits policies can be the place most rife with DEIB issues. For example, many benefits plans cover gender dysphoria therapy for those who feel a mismatch between their gender identity and sex assigned at birth, but they do not cover gender reassignment surgery, which is a huge gap in support for people transitioning genders. Benefits are often seen as overhead. Companies view benefits as necessary to attracting talent, but they don't necessarily use them as differentiators for diverse talent. This is a missed opportunity.

Many technology companies in particular are starting to take advantage of leveraging benefits to differentiate. Expanding parental leave to include people who foster or adopt children, not just birth them. Providing military leave pay that goes above and beyond the employees' current salaries so that they can handle the additional costs of being absent from their families. Providing flexible working hours for people who must make frequent doctor visits for medical conditions or take care of elderly or child dependents. Offering relocation stipends and student loan reimbursement for new college grads who may be the first in their families to go to college and who are struggling under crushing student loan debt. All of these policies can have a significant impact on whether you are able to attract and retain women, people of color, people in the military, or people with disabilities.

Understanding whether and how well your policies support equity internally is only one part of a broader process. Don't overlook the need to evaluate the impact of your policies and practices on how well they serve diverse clients as well.

With so many new technologies shaping how we do business with our customers, it's important to bake in marginalized perspectives from the start. Take voice recognition software as an example. If you're currently using it for identification purposes, have you also developed a protocol for how to handle voice changes over time due to aging, hormone supplements, surgery, and so on? Few things are more frustrating for customers than when they cannot get into their own accounts because some software won't validate who they are. And treating them as if they are a fraud in the validation process will ensure that they take their business elsewhere.

Being proactive about how you can best serve as broad a client base as possible can help you avoid these pitfalls. One way you can do this is to include as many different types of users in prototype testing up front as possible and making sure you have diverse perspectives represented on your product development teams. You can also leverage your internal employees for user input and feedback before you go to market.

## Prioritize What to Address

Once you've done your audit and uncovered potential issues, it's time to prioritize them. It's likely you've identified way more concerns than you have the resources to handle in your first six months, so it's necessary to delineate what effort is required and the level of impact you can expect. A prioritization tool I find useful is to plot each issue in an *action priority matrix*, commonly used in business.

The model in Figure 1.4 was inspired by President Dwight D. Eisenhower's 1954 speech to the Second Assembly of the World Council of Churches, where he talked about how he organized his workload and priorities according to level of importance and urgency. This action priority matrix is a variation of President Eisenhower's organization system, but it uses impact and effort instead.[24]

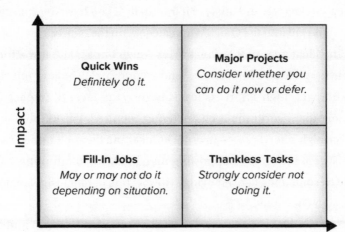

Figure 1.4 **Action Priority Matrix**

By plotting your concerns according to whether they are high or low impact and high or low effort, you give yourself some directional guidance on what to prioritize in terms of Quick Wins, Major Projects, Fill-in Jobs, or Thankless Tasks. For example, you may feel that educating your workforce about DEIB is essential. You might consider it high impact to get everybody on the same page and using shared language around DEIB. However, it could take a significant amount of effort to accomplish this, especially if your organization is very large and distributed.

You might have to invest in online learning modules, external facilitators, and specialized coaching, not to mention travel if you decide to bring people together in person for training. There is also the opportunity cost to consider in taking people away from their job activities to participate in the training. This could be a Major Project. On the other hand, you might want to assess whether employees feel your company culture is inclusive. This might be high impact to help you identify strengths as well as areas for focused intervention across the company. Implementing a survey itself is relatively low effort in that you could develop and analyze it internally if you have the expertise. This would fall into the Quick Wins category on the matrix.

The ideal quadrant is Quick Wins—high impact and low effort— for obvious reasons. But you may end up prioritizing Major Projects— high-impact, high-effort issues—because the level of impact will be more than worth the time and effort required. Fill-In Jobs—low-impact, high-effort issues—may not be ideal, but they may be necessary to ensure that you are supporting marginalized communities. This could be something like removing disrespectful, noninclusive language from your code base.

Some outdated code uses terms like *master* and *slave* to indicate primary and secondary functions, or *whitelist* and *blacklist* to indicate entities that are allowed or denied. These terms are problematic because of their association to the United States' history of racism. Changing deeply embedded code might be considered low impact in that few people will ever see it, and it could be high effort to dedicate resources to implement those changes in huge, legacy systems, putting this into the Fill-In Jobs category. But doing so would send a significant signal to your employees that it matters to use inclusive language throughout your company.

Thankless Tasks are things I conscientiously try to avoid but sometimes find myself inevitably in, despite my best efforts. These are things like ensuring that everyone follows a consistent interview process and documents their decisions in hiring. It's low impact and effort on an individual basis, but it helps ensure that we are putting inclusive hiring principles into practice and mitigating against legal risk, so it is necessary to do.

From these examples, you can see how important it is to get clear on how you define impact. Is it depth or breadth of reach? Is it affecting people in the majority or minority? Is it client facing or employee centric? These are important considerations to define what impact means. By the very definition of DEIB work, you need to prioritize the few over the many, and this can run contrary to how most business decisions get made. In most business decisions, expense ratios are always under pressure to go down while profit margins are under pressure to go up, and this usually translates to prioritizing serving markets with critical mass instead of niche communities. DEIB work often requires the opposite.

## Focus on the Right Things

Which brings us to the idea of the Diversity Equation. Many times, companies focus their DEIB efforts initially on hiring because they see it as the quickest way to increase representation of underrepresented communities. If you don't have any diversity, you've got to add it. However, what I've seen much too often is that retention becomes the key issue.

Companies spend a lot of time, money, and effort to bring in people from diverse backgrounds, but because they haven't spent any time, money, or effort to ensure that they're bringing people into an inclusive culture and environment, all those people they've hired to increase their diversity then leave at roughly the same rate they were hired into the company. So, in reality, you're not making any real progress. In fact, you're actually losing progress when you factor in all the time, money, and effort you've wasted in trying to improve the status quo and getting nowhere:

Hiring – retention = zero progress

How do you figure out if this is your problem? First, look back as far as historical data will allow. Has your representation of various underrepresented groups shifted by more than 3 percentage points over time, or has it remained relatively flat? If you've got at least three years' worth of data to look back on and there hasn't been movement, you have a problem.

If you don't have historical data, then it becomes necessary to look at both your hiring and attrition rates for comparison. Regardless, you need to also interview people who are currently at your company and former employees to better understand their experience and whether you have an inclusion issue to address. This will give you deeper insight into whether you need to address how you onboard people, managers' inclusive leadership skills, career advancement and learning, and/or everything else in between.

One firm I know spent a ton of money and energy recruiting undergraduates from historically Black colleges and universities (HBCUs). The company was quite successful, increasing significantly over time the percentage of Black new college graduates in its annual hiring. Yet, the company was not able to keep these new hires beyond a year when the average tenure at the company was nearly two years. So they knew they had an inclusion issue that needed to be addressed.

Sometimes, these issues have less to do with your company than they have to do with the surrounding community. For example, I spoke with a Black woman who had moved to a Texas town for her role. While her experience within the company was really positive and inclusive, she still felt isolated as one of the few Black people in her town where there was no place for her to easily get the Southern food ingredients that she loved, or to get her hair done by a stylist who knew how to work with Black hair. As a result, she had already decided she wasn't going to stay in her job for long because she wanted to be in a place where she would face fewer struggles to feel like she belonged.

This points to the importance of community development in corporate DEIB efforts. Are you investing in the broader communities in which your company operates, and how are those investments supporting the DEIB of your employees and customers? A friend of mine who used to work at a large technology company shared an example of how to address this. Decades ago, her company opened a facility in Idaho and hired a high number of Black people to work there, but the company found that they were not staying for very long. The company's leaders soon realized that they needed to invest in Black-owned hair salons, grocery stores, and banks to support the growing community with services that would, in turn, support a stronger sense of belonging. As they did so, they saw retention of their Black employees increase. This is just one of many reasons their company is known for its inclusion efforts today, and it's a great example of why we need to focus on the right issues to truly make progress in DEIB.

## Putting It into Action

Interview at least 10 people from various underrepresented groups *who have left the company* within the past year. Some questions to ask:

- What was the primary reason you left?

- What other factors contributed to your decision to leave?

- How inclusive did you feel our environment was? Can you give me some examples?

- What do you think needs to happen to improve inclusion at our company?

- What would need to change for you to come back?

Interview at least 10 people from various underrepresented groups *who are still at the company*, being sure to get a good cross section of job levels, geographies, and tenures. Some questions to ask:

- What were your expectations for diversity and inclusion when you first joined?

- Has the company met or not met those expectations and why?

- How inclusive do you feel our environment is? Can you give me some examples?

- What do you think needs to happen to improve inclusion at the company?

- What would need to change for you to stay three more years?

Summarize key themes. Ask yourself these questions:

- How does this information supplement the data I am seeing?

- What stories did I hear that clearly illustrate some of the issues faced?

- Using the action priority matrix, did the stories I heard change the relative importance or impact of any of my actions?

## KEY TAKEAWAYS

1. Understand basic definitions:

    a. *Diversity* in the workplace focuses on representation.

    b. *Equity* is giving people what they need to succeed.

    c. *Inclusion* is enabling full participation by everyone.

    d. *Belonging* is connecting to people emotionally.

2. We all have bias. What matters is how we mitigate the negative impacts of it.

3. You have to understand why DEIB matters to your organization. Define the problem you are trying to solve so you can get the resources you need to solve it.

4. Audit your data, programs, practices, policies, and norms to determine where your issues are.

5. Prioritizing the right things to work on matters. Don't assume hiring more diversity into your organization will solve everything.

# CHAPTER 2

# Rethinking the DEIB Issue

Ensuring you don't get stuck in the zero-sum game of the Diversity Equation means refocusing on two things: inclusion and equity. When you create a culture and environment that is welcoming and accessible to people of all backgrounds, cultures, and abilities, you will attract more people from underrepresented groups. The more underrepresented people you both bring into and keep at the company, the more people feel like they belong because they see more and more people like themselves working there. This will result in more awareness and advocacy for change to support more underrepresented groups as employees.

This effect gets multiplied when you factor in expanded marketplaces with more diverse customers who demand a deeper level of the services companies offer. Diverse community investment can in turn support employee inclusion, the future talent pipeline, and customer brand loyalty over time as well. Equity becomes the inevitable outcome. I like to refer to this virtuous circle as the *Inclusion Ecosystem.*

# THE FOUR *Ps* OF THE INCLUSION ECOSYSTEM

The Inclusion Ecosystem actually feeds into and sustains itself over time. The ecosystem is made up of what I call the *four* Ps. Because of my background in marketing, I have a penchant for easily digestible acronyms, and this is no exception. You may already be familiar with the four Ps of marketing: price, promotion, place, and product. In DEIB work, I define the four Ps a bit differently (Figure 2.1):

- *People,* which refers to the need to address talent and ensure that they are engaged effectively as individual human beings to thrive and produce their best work.

- *Place,* which refers to both the physical environment people work in and the culture we create in our workplaces. We need culture to be inclusive and physical environments to be truly accessible to all.

- *Product,* which encompasses both products and services— basically whatever a company is selling to make money, and how it is experienced in the marketplace by its consumers.

- *Planet,* which is about the context that we live and do business in. We operate within different communities that are bound by laws and affected by social issues that are constantly changing over time in ways that significantly affect DEIB.

It's important to address all of these different factors for true prog- ress to occur. When we think of DEIB efforts only as talent initiatives, we miss out on the opportunity to capitalize on the synergies between DEIB and business strategies. For example, many of today's technology companies serve hundreds of millions of users globally every month.

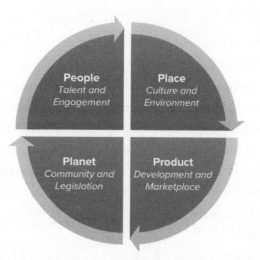

Figure 2.1 **The Four *P*s of the Inclusion Ecosystem**

These companies use sophisticated algorithms that track your content engagement on their sites to determine what content they can serve up to you that you might be most interested in.

However, as a Chinese American woman living in the United States, I have found these algorithms to be a little bit lacking. I have a huge interest in Chinese news and celebrities, but in the earlier days of social media, I was constantly served up only US-centric content, despite my best efforts to click on all things Asian. Or worse, one click on an article about a Bollywood movie, and suddenly all the Asian-oriented articles I saw on my social media feeds were about India. So I raised this issue to one firm's engineering technology leaders, positioning it as an opportunity to increase online engagement by incorporating demographics into the algorithm and ensuring that content could be shared more easily among different countries, including the ability to translate in real time. Being able to recognize this type of problem is why having diverse team members in every aspect of a business, from engineering to product development to marketing to customer service, can help improve someone's experience with the company and ultimately translate to the bottom line.

This example also demonstrates how all the parts of the ecosystem are interrelated and need to be addressed to effectively move the needle forward on DEIB. This company's leaders needed diverse *people* to tell them there was an issue to be addressed and an inclusive *place* in which that issue could be surfaced. The *product* had to be changed to deliver a better consumer experience, and they had to do it in a way that aligned with privacy laws and an understanding of communities across the *planet*.

If we do our job properly, we will also see each of the parts of the ecosystem feed into each other. Creating more educational opportunities for underserved communities will help create your talent pipelines as well as potential clients and markets for the future. As marketplace demand grows, the need to fill it with talent that understands and can work effectively with that market becomes greater, thus driving more inclusive environments and attracting and retaining diverse talent.

One thing I am very explicit about with companies that want to tackle DEIB is that you cannot just address the *people* side and expect to be successful. DEIB affects all aspects of a business, and leaders need to understand how it connects across the four *P*s of the Inclusion Ecosystem in order to drive progress across all of it. Let's dive deeper into each of these *P*s to better understand some of the ways you can address them successfully.

## People

At the heart of DEIB work is *people*. Ensuring that people of all backgrounds have a fair chance at opportunities and are treated with dignity and respect are key parts of the end goal for this work. In the context of the workplace, it's important to think about the entire employee life cycle and what you can do to ensure that people are not excluded at pivotal points of their career journey at your firm. This means examining everything you're doing from hiring to offboarding and looking at ways in which you can create more inclusion at each stage.

To do this, it can be helpful to think of each phase of the employee life cycle as its own end-to-end process. Let's take hiring as an example.

### How Do We Hire People?

Hiring has a lot of different steps to it, and while the details of the hiring process will vary from company to company and role to role, there is a general framework that most hiring processes follow. First, you have to figure out what the role is and the competencies someone needs to fill the role successfully. Then, you have to write the job description. Next, you need to post the job description somewhere that qualified people will see it and apply.

After that, someone who is most likely a recruiter or hiring manager has to screen the applications and/or résumés and determine who seems most qualified to interview. The interview team needs to be chosen and calibrated, and there can be multiple rounds of interviews that candidates must go through. Each round of interviews comes with decision points on who will continue in the process, until someone is extended an offer. There may or may not be some back-and-forth negotiations, depending on your company's policies, until the offer is accepted. Finally, it's time to onboard.

That description was just a high-level overview. When you break down a process into its individual pieces, you will discover there are so many more layers to each step that should be examined as well. One time, I was working with a team tasked with implementing a new *applicant-tracking system* (ATS). This was an opportunity to improve our hiring process by configuring the new ATS to make sure that hiring managers were adhering to a consistent set of steps and not able to bypass the system to hire their best friends. We agreed that we would make it a required step for interviewers to input their interview notes on candidates before an offer could be generated in the system. Seems simple and straightforward as a way to mitigate bias in the process, right?

However, what we agreed to in principle didn't actually happen in practice. The system was in fact set up to require interview notes before an offer, but it was configured only to require the interview notes on the candidate who was receiving the offer, not all the candidates who had been interviewed for the role. That meant we could not objectively compare candidates based on documentation because there wasn't any in the system. Obviously, this hampered our ability to ensure that all candidates were evaluated equitably and fairly against the same set of standards. This was a key lesson for me to really dive deeply into the details of system configurations and process steps to truly understand if they were being set up in a way that supported the DEIB outcomes we were trying to achieve.

It's important to do this so you can identify which steps you want to tackle first, applying the action priority matrix mentioned in Chapter 1 because you can't do everything at once. It would be unrealistic. I've found that methodically addressing each step of the process over time not only helps bring people along on the journey to minimize resistance but also gives you an opportunity to zero in on what changes are making the biggest difference. Isolating variables and testing them one by one to determine what is actually working can take a lot of time, and you'll have to balance that need with making sure your windows of opportunity to drive change don't close while you're doing it. But if you're able to take the time to test what works and what doesn't, you'll be able to make incremental changes in your process that will eventually steer your ship in the right direction.

### How Do We Develop People?

After hiring and onboarding, the next phase of the employee life cycle is development. Let's look at a typical promotion process and how you might test and learn from different interventions. You might identify key steps in the process to be these:

1. Candidates nominate themselves for a promotion by filling out a form.

2. Direct managers review nomination forms and endorse the nomination or not, writing in why.

3. Endorsed nominations are then submitted to the organization's leadership team.

4. Leadership team members review and rank the nominations.

5. Rankings are then consolidated to determine the list of potential promotions.

6. Leadership team members meet to calibrate and decide who gets promoted.

Once you've mapped out your process steps, determine what data you can gather at each step. In the promotion example, you can gather demographic data on who self-nominated, which nominations were endorsed, who received what rankings, and who was promoted, and you can also gather historical trend data on the candidates if you have it. Depending on your analysis of the data, you might conclude that women have not been self-nominating at the same rate as men and that women have not been promoted in proportion to their representation.

In brainstorming potential solutions, you come up with a few ideas, including asking leaders to encourage more women from their teams to self-nominate or changing the self-nomination process to manager evaluations of all employees eligible for a promotion instead. Mapping these in an action priority matrix, you decide that encouraging more women to apply might be a quick win so you design an experiment in which you implement that within one team and compare it to other teams that don't implement this. Measuring who gets promoted as a result of this change in the next cycle will give you data on whether this change is successful or whether you need to try a different solution.

The other area that has to be addressed under the people umbrella is retention. This goes hand in hand with hiring because it takes a huge investment of time and money to hire individuals, so companies want to get a return on that investment in the form of productivity and retention. And you already know from the Diversity Equation that if you don't focus on retention from a DEIB perspective, then you're engaging in a zero-sum game. So what drives retention? According to Gallup research, employee engagement is highly correlated to retention.[1] *Employee engagement* generally refers to how passionate employees are about their job and company. Engaged employees, in contrast to disengaged employees, exert greater discretionary effort and perform at a higher level.

The more engaged employees are, the more likely they are to stay at the company. A sense of belonging and opportunities for development are key drivers to employee engagement. This is strongly aligned with DEIB work because part of our goal is to ensure that everyone—not just those identifying as part of the majority groups at the company—feels they belong. And we need to advance more underrepresented groups into leadership roles to change the status quo.

Which is why allyship education is necessary. Because those in underrepresented groups are developing themselves as leaders, it's important to also have those in majority groups develop themselves as allies to those future leaders. And you should start with the leaders who are making promotion, talent review, and succession plan decisions. They are the ones responsible for the people who were selected to be in the leadership roles you are currently seeing, and it's important to address them first.

While I was at one tech company, we designed a leadership development program for women in senior-level technical roles that very intentionally addressed the role of allies as well. First, we assessed how the women in the program were perceived and what leaders considered their development opportunities. The most common theme we heard was the need for more *executive presence*. Unfortunately, this term is often used as a vague stand-in for needing to act more like a man.[2]

So we designed a program that not only gave our women a stronger support network and specific skill building training but that also included a mentoring component by our senior leaders who were men. This program aspect exposed the senior leaders more directly to all the amazing capabilities and confidence these women were already bringing to the table.

And it paid off as the company went through a round of layoffs. When these leaders were talking through whom to put on the layoff list, none of the women in our program were laid off. In fact, every woman who completed the program and stayed with the company ended up getting promoted or expanding their responsibilities within a year.

## Place

*Place* goes hand in hand with the focus on *people*. After all, it's people who make up a company, and they all have to work somewhere, whether that's physically or virtually, together. Place really comprises two ideas, the tangible and the intangible. The tangible parts are those physical and digital spaces in which people work. The intangible parts are all the behaviors and norms that make up a company's culture. Both must be designed intentionally and nurtured for inclusion and belonging to truly be experienced by every individual.

### Accessibility for All

When we talk about the "physical environment," we're not just talking about the colors on the walls or the furniture on the floors. We're really referring to how accessible the building is to people of all abilities. In the United States, buildings must meet a certain standard that includes being compliant with the Americans with Disabilities Act (ADA). But ADA compliance establishes only a minimum threshold that building designs must meet. And in many cases, that minimum threshold isn't actually practical from a usage standpoint.

As an example, many conference rooms might have built-in electrical outlets in the middle of the conference table or on the floor at various intervals, depending on the size of the room. However, for people with mobility issues who might be using a wheelchair, it can be really difficult and sometimes impossible to plug in their laptop if they can't reach to the middle of the table or if the outlet is located on the floor and they cannot bend down to it. While this conference room might meet the building codes and be convenient for those who are able-bodied, it is certainly not accessible to some folks with differing abilities. Ensuring that you apply universal design to your work spaces will help you create physical environments that are truly accessible to all regardless of age, disability, or other factors.

*Universal design* is designing something so that it can be used by people of all abilities without additional support or modification. It goes beyond ADA compliance in that it is focused on meeting the needs of the greatest number of people possible, not just people with disabilities. Putting electrical outlets a few feet up on a wall where they can be easily reached without bending down would be one way to apply universal design principles to the previous example.

Also, being in the age of innovative technologies that are constantly changing and shaping our world, it's important to note that our environment also includes the digital environment. All companies use technologies to operate their business these days, from mobile phones to videoconferencing to expense reimbursement systems to client relationship management tools. If you don't set a bar for accessibility of the digital systems and services used by your employees every day inside your company, you are missing an opportunity to truly demonstrate inclusion. And employees who aren't able to participate fully in internal events or be productive using your systems means they will be disengaged and they will be more likely to leave.

When you hold all-hands meetings, it makes a huge difference to have an American Sign Language (ASL) interpreter or live closed captioning for those who are deaf or hard of hearing. Having alt-text embedded into images shown on screen are immensely helpful for screen readers to describe those images for people who are blind.

I once worked with an employee who was deaf and had over seven years tenure at the company. But she had participated in all-hands meetings only a handful of times because the process to get live closed captioning for each meeting was so arduous and complicated that it just wasn't worth all the trouble to her. This is not acceptable. We can and should demand better for everyone, whether in tangible ways like ASL interpretation or intangible ways like ensuring that your company's culture doesn't dismiss disability needs at employee events.

### Be Intentional About Culture

As for the culture of the company, if it's not inclusive as I've mentioned before, you're wasting your time and effort on DEIB initiatives. There are some critical ways to nurture a truly inclusive culture. First, make DEIB an explicit part of your company's values. Codifying your commitment to DEIB by communicating that it is foundational to your corporate values provides a serious signal to your employees about what you expect of them.

Second, make sure your leaders are role modeling inclusive behaviors. Your senior executives are setting the example for everyone else to follow. And if they aren't as capable as they need to be, then they need to get the training or coaching needed to help them fulfill that potential.

Third, reinforce inclusive behaviors through rewards and consequences. Performance criteria can highlight inclusive leadership expectations, recognition award categories may include "Inclusive Leader" or "Diversity Champion," and peer-to-peer appreciation notes might have a D&I template. And when someone doesn't behave in an inclusive way, be swift and decisive about letting that person go if they aren't willing to change their behavior.

Most companies have robust policies in place regarding blatant discrimination and harassment that violates their code of conduct, but very few companies actually put in the follow-up work to address microaggressions or other subtle forms of bias that don't rise to the legal definition of discrimination. When those microaggressions go unchecked, it will undermine all your DEIB efforts so it is imperative that employees see that those behaviors get addressed in some way. "Death by a thousand cuts" is often mentioned as a key factor in many underrepresented employees' decisions to leave a company, where the cumulative effect of experiencing microaggressions every day becomes intolerable.

One of the most important ways to support an inclusive culture is through *employee resource groups* (ERGs). ERGs are communities of employees who come together because of a shared affinity or experience and desire to support each other. These groups can go by many different names, including *affinity groups, business resource groups*, or *employee networks*. Many companies have ERGs for women, people who identify as LGBTQ+, Black people, the Latinx community, Asians, parents and more. ERG charters can also vary widely, from being focused solely on community support to doing volunteer work with nonprofit organizations to supporting recruiting to providing feedback on product development. But what they all have in common is a goal to ensure that people from underrepresented backgrounds feel connected to each other and supported in their work lives.

In my experience, most ERGs are underutilized inside companies, which is unfortunate because they can be huge levers to support DEIB efforts across all parts of the ecosystem. But they need to be supported in a way that many companies aren't used to doing. For ERGs to thrive, they cannot be only grassroots, volunteer-run organizations. If DEIB is truly a business priority for the company, then ERG efforts should be treated that way. Like any other business project or initiative, they need executive sponsorship, infrastructure, budgets, and recognition. And in exchange for those resources and support, companies should expect a strategic plan aligned to business goals, metrics for success, and accountability for results from ERG leaders.

Most ERGs don't currently operate this way. I've heard from too many ERG leaders that they are supporting their ERGs as their second or third full-time job and getting burned out in the process. Many ERG members are already burdened with the weight of stereotypes and bias against them, and to ask them to do even more in the interest of the company without the proper support or rewards behind it is just counterintuitive to achieving progress in DEIB.

I know some company leaders may be hesitant to formalize ERGs in this way because they don't have enough resources to provide the right guidance or funding for ERGs, or they fear ERG leaders might feel their autonomy is diminished as a result. I would insist that company leaders not embark on a DEIB initiative unless they are ready to dedicate some level of resources to formally supporting the ERGs in either dedicated head count or budgets. Otherwise, they are setting ERGs up for failure. Once ERG leaders realize that the support from company leaders is genuine and can help them reach their goals of greater representation faster, they tend to embrace their role in supporting the company's DEIB goals.

## Product

If you are able to accomplish your *people* and *place* DEIB efforts well, then you will drive greater ROI to the company on the *product* side. Product is about what you develop and who you are selling it to as a company. Integrating a DEIB lens into your product development process—how you market to your customers and the way you serve your clients—will unlock real value for the company.

But it's only possible if you have people from diverse backgrounds helping to inform and drive those product efforts. And if you don't have people from diverse backgrounds in your company, you are creating your own blind spots to potential opportunities. This can affect your product in many different ways. Let's examine a couple of examples together.

### Diverse Dolls

Mattel introduced a line of dolls called "So In Style," targeted to African-American girls in 2009. Two years before, as the product line was being developed, company executives wanted to be culturally sensitive and asked their African-American employee resource group to help them guide the product launch.

The product line itself was developed and inspired by one of their doll designers, Stacey McBride-Irby, an African-American mother who wanted to create dolls that were more representative of her community.[3] The product line became one of the company's bestselling, minority-focused brands.[4]

### Lights, Camera, Racism

While Mattel got it right when it came to integrating diversity into their product, on the other end of the spectrum is HP's "racist" webcam. Back in 2009, a YouTube video went viral because it depicted a couple of coworkers, one Black, the other white, testing out HP's webcam on the computer. As the white person comes into frame, the webcam tracks and follows her movements. But when the Black person comes into frame, the webcam doesn't move.

This made national headlines, sparking controversy around why and how a camera defect that singles out Black people could exist. HP's company leaders said it was a lighting and contrast issue. Others in the tech community posed the question of whether HP had any Black engineers working on the webcam, whether they tested it out on any Black people before it was released, and how they could have let a product with such a big flaw go to market. It became a PR nightmare for HP.[5] This is the kind of situation that might have been avoided if the company's leadership team had met the previous two conditions in their product development and user research.

———

It's important to ensure that different voices are at the table for product development and market research, and it is crucial to make sure your clients see themselves reflected in your marketing materials and customer service representatives because you will get called out on it eventually.

If you never show people of color in your advertising, you can't expect them to sign up to be your customers. I've had the opportunity to consult with many different kinds of companies over the years. One thing I usually start with is an audit of their customer-facing presence, looking at what kinds of people are part of their website pages, on their social media, and in their marketing outreach. Very often, marginalized communities are barely depicted. So I set about trying to understand why.

Sometimes, companies develop marketing personas meant to represent their target audiences but that are inherently limiting. Other times, they've just never thought about it. Still others say they are focusing on psychographics rather than demographics. Whatever the case, it's important to better understand the impact of your DEIB efforts on your customers. For instance, presentation images can look monolithic if your company's stock photo library does not include people from different backgrounds.

At one company, I had my team curate a selection of stock photos for our brand library to ensure that we could show nonstereotypical images of different family types, people with disabilities, military backgrounds, and other dimensions of diversity in our marketing. This came about when we wanted to share a presentation to a group of military veterans but realized that all our stock photos of people in the military only depicted one branch of service, the army. So that needed to be corrected right away, along with not just depicting people with disabilities as someone in a wheelchair, or seeing only white gay couples in the photo library.

This is not only a consideration for imagery but also for our customer-facing teams. One team I worked with went into a sales pitch with their usual cadre of account representatives who happened to all be male. When they walked into the room, they saw that the majority of people sitting on the other side of the table were women. They were asked whether or not they had any women on their team, and it was an uncomfortable conversation to say the least. In the end, they still got the account, but it was a great lesson on how they needed to always think about what was important to the clients they were pitching to and the diversity they were representing in each pitch they made.

Whether you are in a consumer-facing or B2B company, more and more of your clients are looking at how firms are truly demonstrating a commitment to DEIB. Do you have a multilingual workforce that can address customer service calls from non-English-speaking customers? Have you worked out a protocol to route those customers to the person who can best help them and do it quickly? Do you have customer profiles that don't assume gender or limit name prefix choices to the binary Mr. or Ms.? Are your security questions assuming a certain background or reflecting outdated stereotypes?

At one company, the leaders received an angry email from a client who couldn't open an account for his daughter because a required security question in the process asked for the mother's maiden name. This client was one-half of a gay couple, and it was rightfully upsetting to him that this field was required when it essentially erased one of the parents' relationship with his daughter. In addition to being a very out-dated security question, maiden names can be easily found online if people look deeply enough—that's not very "secure." It took the collaboration of multiple functions, including security, legal, fraud, user experience, and client service teams, to update the form and remove that question. That company now has a much more inclusive and secure account opening experience that makes everyone feel represented.

## Planet

Last but not least, we must consider our role in society and how we contribute to or take away from the well-being of the world we operate within. No person is an island, and neither are businesses. Companies are made up of people, and the decisions made by those people in pursuit of profit will reverberate far beyond the confines of any one company. We recognize this inherently in legislation that limits the environmental impacts of manufacturing companies or wage laws that prevent the exploitation of labor. And studies have shown a link between better financial performance and companies that support environmental, social, and governance (ESG) issues.[6]

Doing good is also good for business and an important piece of how DEIB operates in the broader community as well. *Planet* is really about considering how an organization has a social impact on society and how it can be a force for positive change. If companies do this well, they have the potential to create both more diverse talent pipelines and a broader client base.

Companies can drive social impact in many different ways. Employee volunteering, philanthropy, product donations, and incorporating a social mission into its company goals are all ways to reap the benefits of being socially conscious. Salesforce developed a great 1-1-1 model, which pledges 1 percent of equity, 1 percent of product, and 1 percent of employee time to community efforts.[7] TOMS pioneered the One-for-One business model, where the company donated a pair of shoes to a community in need for every pair of shoes purchased.[8] Nike has pledged $140 million over the next 20 years to addressing racial equality for Black Americans.[9]

Whatever resources you choose to give back to communities, it's helpful to think about how to align them with your DEIB efforts as well. For example, if you are in financial services, devoting resources to improving financial literacy within underserved communities will not only help create more economic opportunity and stability for historically marginalized groups but can also help expand the potential future marketplace for the industry as a whole.

Many companies have a policy of providing paid work time for employee volunteering. Companies I've worked for have provided anywhere between one and five fully paid workdays to volunteer each year. Providing employees with a list of volunteer opportunities in your local communities or with nonprofits dedicated to causes that are aligned with the company's business or DEIB goals can be particularly helpful for those who want to give back but aren't sure how. ERGs can often play a huge role in providing employee volunteer opportunities that fit into the company's DEIB goals. They organize volunteer events, drive community outreach, champion causes important to their communities, and mentor the next generation of talent.

### A Social Reckoning

It's important for large corporations to see and understand how social movements can play a major role in the ways in which you operate and structure your DEIB efforts. One movement that caused many companies to reevaluate their DEIB programs was the Black Lives Matter movement that came to a head during the summer of 2020.

The murder of George Floyd in May 2020 sparked a racial reckoning felt around the world for months after his death.[10] It brought to the forefront the inequitable and often inhumane experiences of Black people, particularly in the United States. Exacerbated by the anxiety and uncertainty of the COVID-19 pandemic, protests against racial injustice and the need for police reform grew to a scale not seen since the civil rights movement in the 1960s and sparked a movement of global solidarity.

As a result, companies made statements against racism and pledged millions of dollars to racial justice organizations. They also allocated more resources for leadership development and efforts to hire underrepresented people of color. The jury is still out on whether companies will follow through on their commitments and whether we will see a greater number of Black people in senior leadership roles as a result. But this was an example of how important it is to align your DEIB efforts with your community efforts. Expectations from employees, shareholders, customers, and legislators have all increased around DEIB efforts, and companies need to be both proactive and responsive to that.

Another critically important area from a planet perspective is legislative advocacy. Some companies will argue that they should not take political positions on social issues like DEIB because it is not central to their business. In my opinion, this is an overly narrow point of view. People do not leave their identities, biases, or beliefs at home when they walk through a company's proverbial front door. People are central to your business, and issues that affect your people's fundamental rights are issues that must be addressed if you want a truly engaged and productive workforce.

All human rights that many of us take for granted now started as a sociopolitical struggle. Working women were guaranteed equal pay for equal work only through the Equal Pay Act of 1963. Discrimination against Black people was outlawed only in 1964 with the Civil Rights Act. And it was only recently in June 2020 that the US Supreme Court affirmed that LGBTQ+ people were protected from workplace discrimination under the Civil Rights Act. Companies that do not take a stand on issues affecting their employees' lives are missing a potential opportunity to create engagement and loyalty.

One case that brought this into sharp focus years ago was a 2008 proposition introduced in California that sought to define marriage as only between a man and a woman.[11] At the time, few companies were willing to take a political stance on social issues. LGBTQ+ employees everywhere asked their companies to make a show of support against the proposition, especially after large, brand-name companies like Apple, Levi Strauss, and Google did so.[12] And yet, a majority of companies adhered to a typical policy at the time of not taking a political stance on social issues. It felt like a mistake back then, and in retrospect, I realize I could have played a bigger role in the various conversations that were happening among my colleagues across industries around how to respond to the legislation and the best way to move forward. Instead, many business leaders tried to navigate a middle ground by making personal public pledges against the proposition and I remember hoping that was enough to sway public sentiment.

When the proposition passed though, many LGBTQ+ colleagues I knew in California were despondent. It was a blow to their fundamental rights as human beings. What happened next was predictable. Some LGBTQ+ employees left their companies, in search of a workplace they felt would be stronger advocates for their rights. Their reason for leaving may not have shown up on any company exit surveys as specifically related to their disappointment but it was clear from the many conversations I had with people in the aftermath of the vote just how negatively the proposition's passing was affecting the LGBTQ+ community. Companies that had not taken a stance had broken their LGBTQ+ employees' trust in them as an organization that cared about all of its employees, and it took years for many LGBTQ+ employees to recover from that.

My lesson learned was to ensure that leaders can see the long tail impact of their decisions to engage or not engage. And that not engaging is *actually* taking a stand, whether you like it or not. Nowadays, more and more companies take stances on social issues because they have recognized this shift in expectations from employees and they see the positive difference they can make by being purpose driven beyond the bottom line.

And you will be faced with these kinds of situations in the future, so it's imperative that you prepare for that. With continued innovations in technology and social media, all of us now have a much bigger window into issues that might have been more hidden from view years ago. Which means both good and bad DEIB behaviors get picked up and amplified much faster and more broadly than ever before, and the pace of this will only quicken over time. So get clear on your values now, have the hard conversations on DEIB issues that you see on the horizon, and agree with your leaders on how you want to handle them proactively. Then you'll be able to respond and advocate in a way that is authentic and true to your brand and supportive of your employees.

## PUTTING IT INTO ACTION

For each *P*, document the work that your company has been doing around that area, answering the questions in Table 2.1. If you have nothing to document for a particular *P*, ideate ways in which DEIB efforts can make an impact in that area.

Table 2.1 **The Four *P*s: People, Place, Product, and Planet**

| People | Place |
|---|---|
| • How is your hiring process inclusive?<br>• What programs are in place to advance underrepresented talent?<br>• Are you measuring employee sentiment on inclusion and belonging? | • Do you have a public statement about your company's commitment to DEIB?<br>• What kinds of ERGs do you have, and what activities do they engage in?<br>• Do you have an accessibility process in place for product development and internal systems? |

| Product | Planet |
|---|---|
| • How diverse is the imagery used in your marketing?<br>• Do you use inclusive language in your communications and technology?<br>• How diverse is your client base, and are your systems and teams set up to serve your clients appropriately? | • How are you supporting employee giving and volunteering in your community?<br>• Have you defined a clear social issues engagement decision framework?<br>• What are your corporate philanthropy and advocacy goals? |

Solicit and share stories that illustrate the issue or impact in each *P*.

Make sure you document your efforts in each area over time to show progress and demonstrate how they overlap.

## CREATING THE CONDITIONS FOR SUCCESS

You can have the best plan in the world, but if you aren't able to execute it, it doesn't matter. Making sure you have enough money and people to actually get your plan done is important, but it's only the first step. Many companies have thrown tons of money and people at DEIB, and yet, these companies are making only minimal progress. Facebook, Google, Apple, and Microsoft have spent millions of dollars over the years on their DEIB initiatives, but their percentage of women and Black and Latinx people are still far away from parity with the US population since they started releasing their representation numbers in 2014.[13]

While there has been some improvement in the number of women in technical roles at these companies, over the course of six years, their representation of Black workers is still only in the single digits. Intention is great, but if it isn't paired with courage, accountability, respect, and empowerment (CARE), it will not move the needle. All employees within a company, especially leaders, need to CARE to make progress in the DEIB space. Let's dive into each of these in more detail.

## Courage

Courage is the foundation needed to drive success in DEIB. Deloitte defines *courage* as one of its six traits of an inclusive leader.[14] Inclusive leaders are not afraid to challenge the status quo. They are willing to take some personal risks and engage in uncomfortable conversations to push people to reexamine their current beliefs and drive real change.

By its very nature, DEIB work means that you as a leader will have to make decisions that support or benefit a minority group rather than the majority group. This usually feels really uncomfortable for people since it runs counter to how we make most business decisions, which usually gives greater weight to the majority. Including transgender surgery or mental health benefits in your company's medical plans is one example of deciding to increase your expenses to support the needs of only a small percentage of your employees, but it sends a much broader signal about your commitment to inclusion that cannot be measured.

Courage also means that you may have to let go of ways of doing things that may have served you well traditionally, like opening up your talent pipeline to include historically Black colleges and universities (HBCUs), Hispanic serving institutions (HSIs), community colleges, and boot camp graduates instead of recruiting from only the so-called top-tier schools. Many people use an education or company pedigree as a proxy for competency and skill. In tech, if you've worked at Facebook, Apple, Amazon, Netflix, or Google (FAANG), chances are good that you'll get an interview. Résumés with the requisite skill sets but not one of these big-name companies on them are often relegated to the second-tier review pile. Really challenging yourself and your colleagues to look beyond certain credentials and define the skills and competencies that make people successful in their roles at the company takes more thought and effort. But making the effort will help you broaden your recruiting efforts as you go looking for talent where others might not.

Supporting DEIB also means confronting people when they are engaging in biased or inappropriate behavior. Your goal is to educate them about how their biases are showing up and help them change their behavior moving forward. One of my colleagues had to talk to a male team leader who would hold meetings at the end of the workday and only ever ask the women in the office to clean up afterward. The team leader wasn't thinking about how he was making his employees who were caregivers choose between being perceived as dedicated employees who stayed late for meetings or picking up their children from school or daycare on time. Nor did he realize that in asking only the women on his team to clean up, he was expressing an unconscious bias toward women as the help.

After the conversation, he was appropriately horrified to realize that he was asking only the women to clean up, but he still had a little trouble understanding that he needed to modify his meeting times to accommodate his staff's other obligations. It took courage for people on his team to speak up about the inequities of their manager's behavior and courage for the manager to admit his blind spots existed.

Ultimately, you are driving change, either in processes, systems, behaviors, or all three. Since people are generally resistant to change, you need to have the fortitude to push against that resistance and stand up for DEIB regardless. And you have to be willing to fail. Increasing diversity in Corporate America is a hard problem to solve. If it were easy, somebody would have solved it by now. This means you will have to try things that have not been done before, and that will take courage. It may not work the first time or even the second time, but as long as you learn from each attempt and keep trying, you'll be moving forward.

## Accountability

The next critical factor for success in DEIB is *accountability*. There is a saying in business that "what gets measured gets done," and in many companies, metrics and results are their mantras. Yet, those same companies are not measuring their DEIB efforts with the same level of rigor as they apply to the rest of their business. Some companies might be afraid of uncovering issues that will be used as evidence of discrimination in lawsuits. Others may worry that if they don't show progress on their numbers over time, it could lead to bad PR, disengaged employees, and upset customers. Still others might worry that the factors contributing to DEIB issues are outside their control and they therefore shouldn't be held accountable for progress.

What I would point out is that whether you choose to diagnose an issue or not, if it's there, it won't go away on its own. Ignoring an issue isn't addressing it. And being silent on an issue is actually being complicit with the status quo that is holding underrepresented groups back. If you truly want to make progress on DEIB, you have to be willing to look at your numbers, share the results with the appropriate people who can actually do something about them, and monitor your progress over time so you can adjust your actions as necessary. Many companies are now recognizing they need more accountability to drive progress, and they are publicly releasing their demographic numbers annually in an effort to be transparent and held accountable. Technology companies in particular are at the forefront of measuring every aspect of their talent processes and culture to determine where there may be differences in experiences across groups and if the changes they are making are truly having an impact.

Beyond organizational accountability we also need to have individual accountability. Individual leaders need to be held accountable for how they demonstrate inclusive leadership. They should all have defined DEIB-related performance goals. And if they are meeting those expectations, they should be rewarded for it. Having leaders set DEIB-supportive team goals and linking those results to their compensation can be a game changer.

In January 2021, Starbucks announced that top executives would be given more equity if they achieved their goal of increasing diversity among its managerial ranks over the following three years.[15] Uber has tied some senior executives' compensation to whether they achieve their goal of increasing women and underrepresented employees in specific roles.[16] In 2015, Intel tied 7 percent of employee bonuses to hiring and retention goals, as part of their diversity objective to reach "full representation" by 2020. In 2018 they achieved it.[17]

A 2016 Harvard study showed that companies do a better job of increasing diversity when they have diversity task forces or managers that have direct responsibility for DEIB initiatives.[18] This reinforces the idea of *social accountability*—that is, our need to look good to others. Just knowing that there are people watching and holding you account-able to your commitment to DEIB can make a difference. At one com-pany, when we implemented a process for reviewing the demographics of employees who were rated high potential and high performance, we found that the diversity among those who were nominated for succes-sion plans increased by up to 40 percent.

## Respect

*Respect* is about having regard for the feelings, wishes, rights, or tradi-tions of others. How it is expressed is at the heart of DEIB progress. You need to demonstrate respect for historically marginalized groups in both deed and word. And that means being mindful of your impact on others by using respectful language, celebrating different cultures and contributions, avoiding cultural appropriation, and creating policies that give room for those with beliefs different from your own.

This can manifest in many ways. Do you have floating holidays available for people with different religious or cultural celebrations? Have you created a private space for those who follow faiths that require prayer throughout the workday? Do you have lactation rooms for nursing mothers to use? Are you refraining from using "guys" to refer to everyone, regardless of gender? Can you comfortably address race in the workplace? These are just a few of the kinds of questions you should be asking during your DEIB audit. When someone in your company brings up how using *insane* or *crazy* marginalizes people with mental health issues, do you try to address it, or do you just brush it off as someone being "too sensitive"? These are the moments when you decide what you stand for and the level of respect you have for those outside of the majority.

We've all heard of the *golden rule* to treat others the way you want to be treated. But respect is really about the *platinum rule* to treat others the way they want to be treated.[19] The platinum rule recognizes that you are not the center of the universe and that when you are dealing with historically marginalized communities, it's a better idea to center the idea of respect around their needs instead of yours. This is where the dynamics of privilege and power comes in.

Many times, people in a majority group assume their own experiences are similar to what everyone else also experienced. For example, a white person who has grown up in poverty and struggled may be offended by the idea that they have privilege. When you remember the platinum rule, you realize that it's not about what you've experienced personally but rather about what other people are experiencing. If a Black person shops in a store and is followed closely by the security guards while a white person shopping at the same store is not, then that white person has the privilege of not being profiled as a potential thief based solely on the color of their skin. And if the security guards applied the platinum rule, they would ask themselves how those Black customers would want to be treated while they shopped, and they might potentially use their power to change their behavior as a result.

Respect means having empathy for others' experiences and taking the appropriate actions based on that empathy. Taking the time to learn about experiences that are different from your own, understanding what motivates each individual on your team, and applying a lens that centers their needs first will help you be a more inclusive leader. All of this is related to proximity as well. The closer you are to a community, the more likely you are to understand their needs and issues and the more likely you are to create a culture and environment that takes those needs into account. Being curious about others allows you to ask the right questions to learn about what's important to them, what barriers they are encountering that need to be addressed, and how to ensure that they feel a sense of belonging.

## Empowerment

The final letter in CARE stands for *empowerment*. One aspect of empowerment is ensuring that all voices can be heard in your company. When employees don't feel they can speak safely about DEIB issues they see, you will miss critical information to act upon. If you don't have clear feedback channels to hear directly from your employees, it will be difficult to understand whether employees have issues with your DEIB initiatives, communications, or lack thereof.

As mentioned earlier in Chapter 1, many companies use regular employee engagement surveys to assess the extent to which employees feel their culture is inclusive and contributes to their sense of belonging. Some companies conduct separate DEIB-focused surveys in addition to standard engagement surveys. Separate DEIB surveys are good for diagnosing whether different groups of employees are having different experiences that need to be addressed. Whether you do these surveys just once a year or more frequently, what's most important is that you actually put the feedback into action and communicate your progress. Otherwise, employees may feel their opinions don't matter at all and stop answering your survey questions honestly.

It's also necessary to have more than one feedback channel. Managers can certainly bubble up what they are hearing from their employees, but you should also ensure that you have things like a code of conduct hotline for people to report issues anonymously, or a suggestion box for people to share ideas for improvement.

Another aspect of empowerment is how you are enabling people whom you've tasked with driving DEIB initiatives at your company to actually do the work. Nothing is worse than asking people to dedicate a portion of their time to supporting DEIB initiatives and then not giving them the power or authority to affect decision-making or take appropriate actions.

I have worked with too many DEIB councils or task forces that have no clear charter or set of responsibilities and are left floundering because they don't know what to do. Not supporting the work of the DEIB councils runs the risk of having these champions be seen as nothing more than window dressing and will ultimately disengage your most meaningful influencers across the company. And before you decide to do any targeted DEIB program at the corporate level, please don't do it without consulting people from the groups who will be most affected.

One example of this was a situation where the leadership team decided to start an external scholarship program benefiting Black university students to pursue careers in the company's industry. Unfortunately, they didn't consult their internal Black employees before rolling out this scholarship. If they had talked to those Black employees first, they would have learned that, while an external scholarship was appreciated, their Black employees felt an investment in leadership development efforts to increase the representation of Black employees in management would have been more meaningful. And so the scholarship was not perceived as meeting the community's needs, which meant the company didn't quite achieve the impact they were hoping for.

Bringing in more entry-level talent would not be impactful if they would not be able to advance into higher levels at the company. When you factor in that the leadership team making the decision was 100 percent white, it felt really disempowering to the Black community that they weren't involved in the decision-making process, and the team missed an opportunity to really engage the community for broader success.

When you care for others, you look after them. When you apply CARE principles, you are creating the conditions necessary to support their well-being inside your company in concrete ways that will help you achieve your DEIB goals.

## PUTTING IT INTO ACTION

Sit down with your leadership team and discuss how you will all align around CARE. Some questions for you to consider are listed in Table 2.2.

### Table 2.2 Questions to Consider in Aligning with CARE

**Courage**
- If a law goes against our code of conduct in the workplace, how will we handle it? How much risk are we willing to take on in order to do the right thing?
- Are we willing to lose customers who don't agree with our stance on social issues?
- What are we willing to change to drive a more inclusive and equitable environment?

**Accountability**
- Are our actions in alignment with our words?
- How will we reward DEIB behaviors in the workplace? What consequences are in place when bad behavior happens?
- Will we call each other out for not challenging the status quo?

**Respect**
- How are we accommodating or celebrating different cultural holidays and celebrations?
- Are our benefits and policies supportive of diverse needs across our employee base?
- Can we have uncomfortable conversations about diversity topics in the workplace?

**Empowerment**
- Are we actively supporting marginalized communities, or are we burdening them to help themselves?
- What channels do we have in place for employees to express their needs and concerns?
- Do we involve impacted stakeholders in our decision-making on DEIB?

## KEY TAKEAWAYS

1. Solving for DEIB goes beyond just talent. It means embedding DEIB in everything a company does.

2. Develop a plan to address the four *P*s of the Inclusion Ecosystem:

   a. *People:* Talent and engagement

   b. *Place:* Culture and environment

   c. *Product:* Development and marketplace

   d. *Planet:* Community and legislation

3. Done well, the four *P*s reinforce and build off of each other, becoming a virtuous circle.

4. To make progress on DEIB, you have to demonstrate CARE:

   a. Courage

   b. Accountability

   c. Respect

   d. Empowerment

5. Remember the *platinum rule*: treat others the way they want to be treated.

# CHAPTER 3

# A Framework for Change

Unfortunately, we are not seeing the kind of progress in DEIB that we should be. Pick an industry, any industry, and look at how many women, racial and/or ethnic minorities, LGBTQ+, and/or people with disabilities are CEOs, represented on boards, or part of senior leadership teams. Tech companies are notorious for slow DEIB progress, but many other industries do not fare any better. Despite decades of DEIB commitment, we are barely making incremental progress. At the rate we are going, women won't achieve pay equity in North America for another 60 years or longer.[1]

That timeline is way too long. I'd rather we fix the DEIB problem before then so that the next generation of DEIB leaders will no longer be needed. Achieving this means we need to do something different from what we've done before. Changing today's status quo will require rethinking our systems, processes, and policies to truly achieve different results. You know that definition of insanity where you do the same thing over and over again and yet expect a different outcome? That is exactly what we are doing here, and it's time to step off the hamster wheel.

# DEIB AS TRANSFORMATIONAL CHANGE

But how do we do that? The most critical thing to understand about DEIB work is that it's all about change. We are trying to change entrenched systems, behaviors, and attitudes. DEIB work needs to be approached as a change process that is managed effectively so that people will adopt those changes. It's one thing to have a great idea and strategy. It's quite another to get people to actually implement them and change their behaviors. Although people are naturally resistant to change, applying a change framework to DEIB is exactly what we need to help us overcome that inertia. Because let's be real. Very few people would overtly object to DEIB work because objecting to it is not politically correct. The issue lies more in a lack of motivation to change. After all, if you're comfortable in and benefiting from the status quo, you would likely not give it up without very good reason.

As with any change process, the first thing you need to do is define the change. This means setting a clear goal. It's important to communicate what you are trying to accomplish with DEIB. I am a big proponent of defining measurable and meaningful goals that you can hold people accountable for achieving. To check whether they are meaningful, ask yourself if they are high impact and relevant to you, your company priorities, and other key stakeholders. Measurable can be either quantitative or qualitative, but it must be a clear definition of what success will look like and be tangible with an explicit time frame. It's all right to revisit these results and adjust them as conditions change, but you've got to set something down initially to provide people with the right direction and accountability. I find when people follow the formula below for defining goals as key results, they are much crisper and more memorable:

**Result statement:**
action + target audience + measure of success

It helps to state results simply, with a concrete metric, so that people will find it easier to remember and more compelling to take action on. Here are a few examples of some goals to get you started:

- *Hiring result:* Increase hiring rate for women at the firm by 3 percent YoY.

- *Development result:* Increase hiring and promotions of underrepresented racial and/or ethnic groups at executive levels to reach parity with overall representation in three years.

- *Culture result:* Increase inclusive leadership behaviors across all employees to yield no statistically significant differences between underrepresented groups and majority groups in employee engagement by 2023.

It's also important for you to define results for your team that are aspirational enough to stretch people's thinking around what they can do but also realistic enough to be achievable, because the last thing we want to do is demotivate people with a lack of progress. It's also important to set the right level of expectation around progress in this space. You are on a journey that won't reach its goals overnight. Some things like leadership representation will take time to change because you can only promote a small percentage of people in a year. Other things like increasing hiring rates of URGs can change quickly, particularly if you are on a high-growth curve and hiring people at all levels of the company. The progress you make depends on both the maturity of your business and the dedication of your leadership to the cause.

As you think about the goals you want to achieve in DEIB, you need to ground them in guiding principles—strategies and actions that are demonstrably different from what is happening today. I always ask leaders to develop a DEIB action plan based on their assessment of their organizations. Need examples? Some tangible ways you can support DEIB through various talent initiatives are described in Table 3.1.

**Table 3.1  Examples of DEIB Goals, Guiding Principles, Strategies, and Actions**

|  | Hiring | Leadership Development | Inclusive Culture |
|---|---|---|---|
| Goal | Achieve a 3% increase in hiring rate YoY for women at the firm. | Achieve parity with overall racial and/or ethnic representation at executive levels in 3 years. | See no statistically significant differences between underrepresented groups and majority groups in employee engagement by 2023. |
| Guiding Principle | Talent is evenly distributed; opportunity is not. | The best talent equals the most diverse talent. | Inclusion is intentional, not organic. |
| Strategy | Require that at least two fully qualified women have been interviewed for each role. | Evaluate all eligible talent for promotion opportunities to the director level and above. | Tie people managers' merit raises and/or bonuses to performance ratings on inclusive leadership. |
| Actions | The senior leadership team increases speaking engagements at events for women, and the recruiting team adds new women-focused organization partnerships for sourcing pipeline. | An executive mentoring program is launched and available to all racial and/or ethnic minority talent at senior manager level and above. | All people managers take training on how to be an inclusive leader, and they have opportunities to take advantage of coaching and practice on this topic. |

## Applying Change Management

When you're attempting the kind of transformational change that DEIB necessitates, you should also consider applying a change management process to your work to support successful adoption. There are many change management models out there, and one I am partial to is the ADKAR model (*awareness, desire, knowledge, ability*, and *reinforcement*) by Prosci.[2] I like this model because it is based on the premise that organizations only change when individuals change, and it offers a clear, structured process to do that. This work needs to start internally. Everyone needs to understand both their connection to and responsibility for DEIB. We all have a role to play in supporting a culture of inclusion within our organizations.

The ADKAR model is simple. It spells out the concrete outcomes that people need to achieve for change to stick:

- *Awareness* of the need for change

- *Desire* to support the change

- *Knowledge* of how to change

- *Ability* to implement the change

- *Reinforcement* to make the change stick

Our first two chapters tackled the first phase of the ADKAR model—*awareness of the need for change*—but awareness is the easy part. Generating *desire to support the change* is much harder. There are a couple of key strategies I have used to tackle this: *integration* and *influence.*

Rather than add DEIB to the list of things people have to do, I've found it's better to *integrate* DEIB into the business's priorities. Need to hire 1,000 people in the next year? Make sure you create the most inclusive hiring process possible. Need to overhaul your antiquated client management system? Include fields for pronouns used, military branch and rank, and accommodation needs. It's important to look for opportunities in the business where you can integrate DEIB into the strategic agenda to lower barriers to inclusion.

Whenever I've gone into a company either as a consultant or employee, I've very intentionally aligned my DEIB work to the company's most critical priorities. When I interview senior leaders about their DEIB needs, I don't actually start with questions specific to DEIB. I start by asking what their highest business priorities are. Then I ask what their people strategy is to help them achieve those priorities. This gives me key insight into how DEIB can be integrated into their priorities and strategies.

If it's your retail network that brings in 40 percent of revenues, you can bet I'm talking to leaders in that department first about how DEIB can help them increase their revenue share. If your firm's top priority is to undergo a digital transformation of all product lines to better serve the heightened expectations of consumers for everything to be instantly accessible online, then I'm reaching out to the firm's top engineering and product management leaders to ensure that they're incorporating a DEIB lens into their digital development process.

On top of that, I always talk to the finance leaders. DEIB is typically underresourced in companies, and the finance function holds the power to unlock the dollars needed to truly make progress. It's critically important to understand how financial decisions are made, what factors are accounted for in their financial models, and where money flows through the organization in order to leverage these aspects to support DEIB. Lastly, you absolutely need to partner effectively with the legal department. They can help you position your DEIB efforts as ways to effectively manage risk for the company and keep your efforts within legal boundaries. Contrary to popular belief, some of my biggest supporters of DEIB have been in the legal department.

You also need champions and *influencers* to sponsor the change across all the different phases of change management, from preparing for the change to managing the change to reinforcing it. Having the right influencers supporting DEIB will make or break your ability to drive the changes you are making. First and foremost, make sure your CEO is on board. Everyone in the organization takes their cues from the CEO, and if the CEO isn't visibly communicating about your DEIB efforts, then people will likely draw negative conclusions about the company's level of commitment to it. Second, choose whom to tap beyond the CEO for support of your initial DEIB change efforts carefully.

Ask these questions: What business lines are driving the most revenue for the business or are the most critical to positioning the company for future success? Who are the most respected leaders with an inherent passion for DEIB who already have a long tenure behind them or are in critically important roles for future succession plans? What internal functions have the most power in terms of supporting or challenging DEIB efforts? Knowing the answers to these questions will help you determine who can help accelerate your efforts the most across the business.

Throughout my career, I've made both good decisions and bad decisions when it came to choosing influential sponsors. One of my biggest mistakes was focusing solely on C-level executives inside the company to sponsor our employee resource groups. In particular, our employee resource group focused on LGBTQ+ employees needed an executive sponsor. Unfortunately at the time, the company did not have any out LGBTQ+ C-level executives.

So I had to decide whether to find an executive sponsor at a lower job level and risk not having an advocate with a direct line to the CEO or to go with a non-LGBTQ+ C-level executive who felt they could advocate effectively for the community nonetheless. I went with the latter. This turned out to be a mistake. Because the executive didn't have a strong connection to the LGBTQ+ community, he didn't engage as deeply as I had hoped he would. The ERG leaders would meet with him on a regular basis, but he did not actively participate in their events, and he wasn't comfortable representing their point of view on LGBTQ+ issues. The ERG's leaders began to turn over, and their level of activities started to decrease.

It was clear the ERG needed someone from the LGBTQ+ community as their sponsor to help them feel like they had a champion. When an out LGBTQ+ vice president agreed to sponsor the ERG, and we created a forum for those at the C-level to hear from our ERGs on a regular basis, we were able to turn things around and the LGBTQ+ ERG began to thrive again.

This, however, doesn't mean that you always must have someone from within a community as that community's champion. Some of the strongest champions and influencers we've had for DEIB and ERGs have been allies rather than people who are in a particular underrepresented group.

For example, I've had men be executive sponsors for women's ERGs, and that has turned out to be one of the most effective moves we could have made to support more women being hired and advancing inside the company. With a male executive's sponsorship of one company's women in technology ERG, we were able to elevate our recruiting efforts at a major women's technology conference to increase our hiring from the event by a multiple of seven, as well as launch a global career development week that included mentoring, leadership skill building, exposure to different career paths, and internal recruiting fairs to support women's career advancement. Because this executive sponsor had strong women in his life, including daughters, he was motivated to remove barriers to women's success in the workplace. What matters most is creating an emotional connection to the cause among those who can influence DEIB success.

The third phase of ADKAR, creating *knowledge of how to change*, can be done in multiple ways. One approach I find useful is focusing on small, incremental changes as opposed to big, sweeping ones. It is much easier to get people to make a seemingly minor adjustment to a process than it is to convince them to replace the entire system. In many cases, it takes only small changes in experience to drive big DEIB results that benefit everyone. And driving a real workplace culture of inclusion depends on those experiences creating an authentic sense of belonging for everyone.

One example of a small change is asking employees to add pronouns to their email signatures or other online profiles, and doing it yourself too. This is a very simple and easy thing to do that takes little to no effort other than typing in a few extra words. Yet, it signals so many important things.

By including your pronouns in your email signatures and online profiles, you are showing your solidarity with the LGBTQ+ community, particularly the transgender community, and signaling that your workplace embraces people across the spectrum of gender identity and sexual orientation. You are also indicating that you and your company will not make assumptions about people's gender identity based on their names alone, saving both employees and clients from the potential embarrassment of being addressed by the wrong gender. This is also something that anyone with a gender-neutral or unfamiliar name based in a foreign language will appreciate.

When you combine this change with other LGBTQ+ inclusive efforts, such as adding "cisgender man or woman," "transgender man or woman," "nonbinary," or "third spirit gender identity" options to your HR systems, or additional prefix options like "Mx." in addition to "Mr." or "Ms." to client event forms, you are profoundly transforming the experiences LGBTQ+ people are having with your firm. Small changes like these help to support a more LGBTQ+ inclusive culture.

As you make more and more of these incremental changes over time, they start to accumulate in their impact, and before you know it, you've made a wholesale shift in your organization's culture.

Keeping changes simple also increases the likelihood that they will be adopted. Supporting people's *ability to implement the change* is important too. It's not always easy to apply new DEIB knowledge. While you might be committed to the cause, changing long-held beliefs and habits requires a willingness to examine your old assumptions and make trade-offs that serve both your business's needs and the need to have integrity with your inclusion values.

For example, suppose you have a critical deliverable deadline that's coming up in four months, and you need to hire three people to fill out your team. Because it can take a month or more for new sourcing pipelines to start to yield potential candidates, you may feel pressured against taking time to network and find candidates from underrepresented groups. However, if you believe it's just as important to demonstrate your commitment to DEIB as it is to meet your deadline, then you may choose to spend some budget to hire recruiting contractors or an external search agency to help you increase the number of diverse candidates in your pipeline and give you the best chance of meeting both your objectives.

The goal is to consider the circumstances and ensure that all other options have been exhausted before you decide to do something that might run counter to your DEIB commitment. This is how you incorporate DEIB into your day-to-day decision-making and start to reinforce DEIB skills and knowledge.

As the next phase in the change management process, *reinforcing the change* means being transparent not just about your goals but also about your progress toward those goals. I acknowledge that there is some legal risk in being transparent. And you might risk disappointing people if you don't reach the goals. But I maintain that you cannot run a business effectively without holding people accountable to business goals, and if DEIB is truly a business priority, it should be held to the same level of accountability and visibility as any other business priority.

If you're afraid that people will talk about how low your representation of certain demographics is, I have news for you: they're already talking about it, just not out in the open. People from underrepresented groups already know how low the numbers are. All they need to do is have a look around them or count the number of people in their employee resource groups or networking circles. When you don't share your numbers, people know you're hiding something. And when you do share your numbers, the amount of goodwill and effort you will get from people who want to help make things better will far outweigh the downside.

More often than not, I've seen individuals feel more connected to a firm if they believe that the effort to drive change and create more diverse and inclusive environments is sincere and authentic. But remember that as with any business, you need to set guidelines on who can see what level of DEIB-related data inside your company to protect individual privacy.

## Assessing Change Impacts

The next area of change management that is crucial to implement is understanding the various impacts of the changes you are proposing. Who will be affected by the change? What are the upstream and downstream implications of this change? What new behaviors, mindsets, or processes will implementing this change require? Taking the time to assess these questions and plan for how to address the answers will help you translate systemic, organizational changes down to the individual level and give you a better chance at getting people to successfully adopt those changes. It can also help you uncover blind spots before they become issues or barriers to progress.

At one company I joined, the organization decided to implement a new applicant-tracking system (ATS), as the existing one was outdated. This was an opportunity to configure the new ATS in a way that supported DEIB. For instance, requiring a job description review to identify and remove biased language before a job could be posted was a new protocol we implemented to attract more candidates from diverse backgrounds to apply for roles at the firm.

We did a good job configuring the ATS to support the behaviors we wanted when vetting candidates. However, we did not do the change impact analysis, and therefore, we missed rolling out a change plan that would address the new behavioral changes that current hiring managers needed to make to support these new ATS processes. Not surprisingly, hiring managers found creative ways around the ATS, such as changing job descriptions after they had been approved, thereby resisting the change and undermining our DEIB efforts. This was a key lesson learned about the need to understand change impacts beyond the technology side to really focus on the people side when it comes to DEIB.

This experience also highlights the need for resistance management in any change management process. In DEIB work, there will always be resistance. Human beings possess such a broad spectrum of beliefs around every aspect of life that there is no possible way any DEIB actions will make everyone happy. Given that at its core, DEIB work is about correcting power imbalances, someone will inevitably be unhappy about the prospect of giving up some of their perceived power.

So it's important to prepare for this. There will be a backlash from those who think you are going too far as well as from those who think you are not going far enough. Some people might say that it's better to wait to see what happens and then address the resistance or backlash, so you don't waste precious energy preparing for something that may not happen. I personally think it's better to be proactive in managing resistance to prevent derailing as much as possible. The energy it takes to be prepared is far less than what you would have to expend dealing with fallout from a bad DEIB initiative rollout.

After Google released its demographic data publicly and pressure grew for other companies to follow suit, I have been part of many conversations inside companies about whether to release their data, when to do it, and what to include. In every conversation, it was important to consider potential resistance at every stage of the process. I knew the biggest resistance would come from our legal partners, who were concerned about people leveraging our diversity data to justify discrimination claims. So we made sure we didn't just share our data, but we also shared all the work that had been done to support closing representation gaps and the plans we had to continue elevating our efforts in the future. And we made sure leaders across the company knew what we were releasing and how to respond to questions from employees. This helped us all move forward together.

## PUTTING IT INTO ACTION

Develop a set of clear result statements using the template in Table 3.2. Try to keep the number in the range of three to five results.

Table 3.2  **Creating Your Result Statements**

| Action | Target Audience | Measure of Success | = Result |
|---|---|---|---|
|  |  |  |  |
|  |  |  |  |
|  |  |  |  |
|  |  |  |  |

For each result, document the guiding principle, strategy, and actions you will take to achieve it in the template in Table 3.3.

Table 3.3 **Drafting Your Action Plan**

| Result statement: | | |
|---|---|---|
| Guiding principle: | | |
| Strategy: | | |
| **Actions** | **Timing** | **Owner** |
| | | |
| | | |
| | | |

Looking at your new DEIB plan, use Table 3.4 to apply the ADKAR model to develop a change management plan to address change impacts and potential resistance.

Table 3.4 **Developing a Change Management Plan**

| Awareness | Desire | Knowledge | Ability | Reinforcement |
|---|---|---|---|---|
| Why is the change necessary? | How can you motivate people to adopt the change? | How will people learn to adopt the change? | What is needed to help people implement the change? | How will you make the change stick? |
| | | | | |

# MEETING PEOPLE WHERE THEY ARE

As with any change, you'll also want to think through how to get people at all levels of the company engaged in your DEIB initiatives, particularly decision makers at the top. A former head of DEI at a large global company shared with me her approach to conversations with C-suite executives and other senior business leaders. She would intentionally choose to have these conversations in either small group settings or one-on-one conversations.

Most of these conversations revealed two motivational tracks. Either the executives were encouraged (read: required) to meet with her as part of the company's commitment to DEIB, or they sought her out to learn more about what their role could or should be. In both cases, the end goal was the same: how do they as senior leaders and influencers engage around DEIB so that they, their company and employees, can be more successful?

The biggest DEIB problem they faced was lack of engagement from leaders. They often didn't connect the dots between an inclusive culture and company success. It wasn't about showing up at the next employee resource group event. It was about taking the time to understand the value of inclusive leadership and building a personal and professional brand that served to influence others across the company toward a more equitable environment.

Her initial objective in these conversations was to quickly determine the mindset of the people she met with. What did they think about DEIB? How did it affect them personally or their success as leaders? How did they show up as inclusive leaders? Why did DEIB matter to them? During her conversations, she sought to reframe DEIB as a business accelerator, as opposed to the right thing to do. In order to drive change, she found the most success tapping into what motivates leaders in a business or company setting: How does it tie back to revenue, customer success, market growth? How does it tie back to their professional growth?

She encouraged leaders to look at DEIB through a business lens and to understand that, much like business, they were playing the long game. It required planning, forecasting, and motivating their teams. If they looked at DEIB as a short game, then it would be much harder to realize the results. She reminded them that their people bring in social and societal expectations, as well as other "norms" to the workplace. They couldn't ask people to leave who they were, what they believed, or what they had experienced at the door. Telling people to leave themselves at the door just invites poor performance and productivity.

One example from her experience involved a leader who ran a 640-person enterprise sales organization. When they met, she reviewed his employee roll-up data. His data revealed 95 percent men and only 5 percent women across his organization. When she pointed this out to him, he exclaimed, "Wow. I never knew. I had no idea."

Her next question was, "Are you hitting your sales numbers?"

He said no, to which she said, "Well, how can you hit those numbers with half a sales force?"

He didn't understand. She explained that by having only men in the outbound sales team, he was missing out on an entire network of influencers, relationship builders, and negotiators. She shared her data showing that more women in the workforce are college educated than men, that they are more inclined to maintain deeper ties with former colleagues, school mates, and friends, and that they tend to be master collaborators.

They then looked at his employee satisfaction survey results, which showed 82 percent of men in his organization were satisfied versus only 51 percent of women. Referring to the women, he asked her, "What's wrong with them?"

She looked at him and said, "Why don't you ask them?"

This leader eventually left the company because he was not meeting his sales goals.

My colleague's story illustrates the implications of not focusing on DEIB. Successful change requires engagement across all levels and functions within an organization. You need buy-in and action from the top ranks; otherwise, you will never get the attention and resources you need to move the needle. But you also need energy and input from the grassroots level, so that you can create momentum and ensure that you're engaging in actions that help rather than harm your underrepresented groups. How do you get buy-in from each of these levels? And what do you need to do about what's often referred to as the *frozen middle management layer* in between?

## Top Down

Engaging leaders within your organization may require leveraging several different kinds of elements, depending on what your company's culture most heavily emphasizes. Data and research in the business case may be enough to convince some leaders that they need to engage in DEIB. For others, it may be how you build a relationship and emotional connection to DEIB through storytelling and trust. For still others, it can depend on how strongly you can integrate DEIB actions into leaders' business priorities and make this work as low lift as realistically possible. It's up to you to find out what's most important to your leaders and connect DEIB into that.

Most of the time, I find that leaders have already bought into the concepts of DEIB. What they lack is a clear understanding of how to make progress. Taking no action at all is considered safer than taking the wrong actions that might cause controversy or inadvertently offend someone. What this means is they need a clear road map of actions to take. This can take the form of a customized DEIB action plan that includes a data dashboard supporting your recommended areas of focus. Or it can be a more generic set of suggestions that any leader across the organization can take, such as stating publicly on social media that they are committed to DEIB and looking for ways to get closer to different communities.

What's most important is to define a set of actions that are concrete enough to move the firm toward its defined DEIB goals. Simple advice such as "hire more people of color" is not that helpful because the organization would be doing that if they already knew how to do it well. It's the fact that they don't know what to do that we need to pay attention to. So I try to give leaders easy, concrete actions that they can do to be a champion of DEIB, such as these:

- *Audit your networks.* If it is not diverse, start following and connecting with people from diverse backgrounds. For every new connection you make that is in the majority, invite another connection that is not.

- *Educate yourself.* Either read articles or books, listen to podcasts, or attend webinars on DEIB. Actively participate in trainings offered by your employer.

- *Communicate your support.* When you post a job, explicitly state that you encourage people from diverse backgrounds to apply. Talk to your teams about your commitment to and expectations of DEIB.

- *Amplify minority voices.* Give credit to ideas shared by underrepresented groups in meetings. Share social media posts from underrepresented talent.

- *Make space.* Invite people who haven't spoken during a meeting to share their thoughts. Make sure event speakers are representative of diverse backgrounds.

- *Show up.* Attend ERG events whether you have an affinity for that ERG or not. Listen and learn.

- *Seek input.* If you're leading an initiative that will impact an underrepresented group, make sure you're involving their perspective in it as early as possible.

This is not an exhaustive list by any means, but it contains a few basic ideas that I have found to be helpful guideposts for leaders who are seeking to demonstrate their DEIB commitment. Of course, it's not enough for leaders to show their top-down commitment and role model inclusive behaviors. It must also be coupled with employee support for DEIB initiatives to truly take hold.

## Bottom Up

In a typical corporate hierarchy, the employees are at the bottom of the pyramid whereas the executives are at the top. And while employees form the majority at companies, they often have the least amount of formal power. But they can still be a powerful influence at the company, especially with the rise in employee-driven activism. Technology enables community organizing so much more easily now than in the past. If your company focuses on employees first, then it's important to find ways to engage employees across the company to support DEIB initiatives. Not everyone has to be a champion, but everyone does at least have to not be a blocker. Here are some ideas you can consider, and we'll dive into each in more detail in later chapters.

Consider launching employee resource groups (ERGs), which we described initially in Chapter 2. In larger companies, you may see ERGs focused beyond race and gender on early-in-career professionals, people with disabilities, and people with military backgrounds, among others. In smaller companies, oftentimes there are not enough people to form a group around each affinity separately and so an ERG may manifest as cross-cultural or as a broad inclusion or diversity committee for the firm. ERGs are great ways for employees to activate around driving DEIB goals.

Similarly, many companies launch broader *diversity councils*. You might have an *executive diversity council* that oversees all DEIB initiatives at the company, or you might have an *ERG advisory council* that specifically supports the ERGs. Or you could even have different DEIB *task forces* embedded within different business units and functions to support implementing DEIB action plans. In fact, many companies have all three, depending on their size and objectives. These are all great ways to get employees at all levels of the company engaged in supporting DEIB. When you have multiple workstreams that each of these entities is responsible for, as well as a recognition and rewards system to reinforce grassroots involvement in DEIB efforts, you begin to multiply the effects of each council, ERG, or task force you form by exponential bounds.

Another great way to get people involved is to hold competitions in which people can submit ideas to solve a DEIB problem. Many people are very competitive, and with the right incentives in place, you can drive broad participation in these kinds of activities. In tech, these are often branded as *hack-a-thons*, during which you give employees a short period of time, anywhere from one to three days, to work on problems they've identified and come up with a minimum viable product or solution to address it. This concept originated around computer programming, but it has now been co-opted into a myriad of other areas, including DEIB.

At one tech company, we did a "hack the culture" event where we asked employee teams to come up with a solution to a cultural issue the company needed to address. Teams were asked to pitch their ideas for only five minutes, including Q&A, to a panel of senior leaders in front of the entire company. Employees were also given the chance to vote for their favorite projects. The leaders chose the handful they wanted to fund and implement. Employees eagerly participated because they coveted the opportunity to showcase their ideas and work to senior leaders, the bragging rights if they got chosen, and the chance to actually turn their ideas into reality and address the issue they identified.

The winning pitch was a career development program for women that matched mentors to mentees in the organization based on questionnaires and a fairly sophisticated matching algorithm. This gave way to our *mentor matching program*. While anyone could participate, it had particular emphasis on encouraging people from underrepresented groups to become both mentors and mentees.

Programs like these help employees feel empowered to come together and support the issues they care about. When employees are engaged in developing solutions to problems they see, they are more likely to implement them and to feel that progress is being made. And if they are able to build a community of support around them so they don't feel isolated or feel like they are the only ones who care, they're more likely to feel they are in a place they belong. But while having both top-down and bottom-up approaches will start to make incremental progress in DEIB, I've found that when middle management isn't bought in or held accountable to driving DEIB, it's almost impossible to transform your company's culture to be fully embracing of DEIB.

## The Frozen Middle

We need to talk about the layers in between executives and employees—basically all the people, or *middle managers*, as they are often referred to, who manage other people. How do we get them involved in supporting DEIB? I have found that a combination of setting the right expectations along with accountability mechanisms, as well as creating opportunities for training and deliberate practice, is key to engaging managers in DEIB work.

Managers are the focus of our attention because they are the linch-pins that drive employee productivity and loyalty to the company. According to global analytics and advice firm Gallup, people leave managers, not companies. In their study, one out of every two employees said they had left a job to get away from a manager.[3] So we need to equip managers with a skill set to support and manage a diverse team effectively.

When leaders are up front about their commitment to DEIB and set an expectation that all managers at the company must engage in nondiscriminatory behavior and demonstrate inclusive leadership skills, it holds managers accountable. As leaders set DEIB goals for their organization, managers need to translate those into their own goals for the period. Leaders should also hold regular operating reviews of how their organization is doing against their goals with their managers so that everyone has shared understanding and accountability for progress or the lack thereof.

Depending on their experience level, managers are also often ill-equipped to handle difficult conversations about DEIB or manage across differences effectively within their teams. It's imperative to offer training in inclusive leadership skills for managers as part of an overall manager development program. These inclusive leadership skills can be integrated into an existing manager effectiveness curriculum or taught separately as stand-alone modules, but they should align with your overall management philosophy.

It can also be helpful to do an assessment of inclusive leadership behaviors prior to the training, just to understand what level of capability your managers are currently functioning at. It can give you a better idea of what you need to do to shore up those capabilities, and it can prompt some interesting discussion among teams about different leadership styles and how to bridge them.

Another fundamental way to support and engage managers is to provide deliberate practice hours and individualized coaching opportunities. No one gets better at anything without deliberately having to practice it first. In his book *The Talent Code*, author Daniel Coyle details how deliberate practice helps to unlock great talent.[4] Giving managers the opportunity to practice new inclusive leadership skills within a controlled environment with constructive feedback that they can apply immediately increases their chances of a successful dialogue with employees on DEIB issues. Likewise, having coaching available to support manager efforts to reflect on deeply held beliefs and biases can support the inner work they need to do to unpack their behaviors and reinforce change.

It's also important to realize that despite your best efforts, you may not get everyone on board, and that's OK. At the end of the day, there will always be some segment of people who don't agree with how you're driving change in DEIB at your organization. But if you're able to get a majority of leaders, managers, and employees on board with your DEIB plan and supporting the changes you are driving, then you're likely to see progress over time.

## PUTTING IT INTO ACTION

Using the template in Table 3.5, list stakeholders. Next to each one, write down at least one engagement strategy:

- What is their current mindset about DEIB?

- What are their concerns?

- How will you address them?

Table 3.5 **Stakeholder Engagement Plan**

| Stakeholder | Current Mindset | Engagement Strategies |
|---|---|---|
| Employees | | |
| Managers | | |
| Leaders | | |

## KEY TAKEAWAYS

1. Define the key results you're trying to achieve. Make sure they're focused on outcomes, not activities. Result statements should be measurable, meaningful, and memorable.

2. DEIB work is about driving change, so approach it that way. Applying a change management framework can help you effectively influence and manage resistance so that people will adopt your changes more quickly.

3. Develop a set of concrete actions based on defining inclusive experiences for your employees and customers. Remember, small changes can add up over time to big results.

4. Gaining buy-in from both the top and bottom levels of your organization is important to sustaining momentum and driving progress in DEIB.

5. Managers are a key lever you can pull to support your DEIB strategies. Give them the right expectations, accountability mechanisms, and safe spaces to learn and hone their inclusive leadership skills.

## CHAPTER 4

# Implementing Inclusive Talent Strategies

Once you've gotten everyone at your company on board and have a clear understanding of how leaders, managers, and employees at all levels feel about DEIB, the next step is to dive into your talent strategy and evaluate how you can weave DEIB into how you manage your talent pool. Let's break this down according to the areas where bias can have some of the biggest impact: hiring, performance reviews, and career development.

## INCLUSIVE HIRING

A chief people officer (CPO) at a startup shared a story with me about how her company's inclusive recruiting campaign went viral and kickstarted their inclusion transformation. She was the only woman and only minority on an executive team of eight at a high-growth tech firm in San Francisco, and she described her existence as both wonderful and lonely. Wonderful because as the head of human resources, the leadership team gave her full ownership and empowerment to help implement attraction, engagement, and retention programs for the company. Lonely because she felt she was the only one who didn't look or act like them.

One of her main goals at the time was to hire and retain more people from diverse backgrounds because she felt Silicon Valley was too homogeneous, where the uniform was typically a hoodie with jeans and a pair of Allbirds sneakers. She really wanted to change the stereotypical image of a Silicon Valley worker and break through some of the common barriers that people who don't fit the profile face, like the glass ceiling for women aspiring to be executives, the broken rung at the bottom of the career ladder for entry-level women professionals, and even the bamboo ceiling for Asians.[1]

In 2015, her company needed to double their head count. With many ideas but little time, they chose three strategies to support their hiring efforts:

1.   Increase referral program bonuses to pay out more money than ever before to incent their own employees to recruit by sharing job openings with their networks.

2.   Increase advertising on social media platforms to blast out their hiring messages to the world, encouraging people to join their team.

3.   Create a recruiting campaign, taking over all transit billboards in the transportation hubs of cities like New York or San Francisco, where ridership is high, to broadcast that the company was hiring.

What she thought was a simple recruiting campaign turned into one of the most significant forces that would single-handedly move the needle on diverse representation within their company. More on this later.

## What's in Your Control

Your company says it wants to add diversity to its workforce, but wanting something to happen doesn't necessarily make it happen. To build an inclusive team, your organization needs to examine each piece of the hiring process from end to end with the intent of removing as many barriers to inclusion as possible. Hiring managers especially need to do more "perspective taking" and view the hiring process through the lens of people not like themselves, in order to identify areas where bias may be preventing people with diverse backgrounds from joining your company.

So how exactly do you hire inclusively? In addition to sourcing candidates from diverse pipelines and deploying recruiting strategies to get them to consider your firm, here are five things within your control that you can modify in your hiring process to support attracting and hiring underrepresented candidates.

### 1. Write a Succinct and Unbiased Job Description

If you want a diverse set of candidates to apply for open positions, you have to be very intentional about what you put into the job descriptions. Are you thinking about things like whether your language is unintentionally appealing to one group over another, or whether the qualifications you list are truly requirements?

Many times, we include *preferences* like industry experience or educational backgrounds, but we present them as requirements. If they are truly optional, state that explicitly. Too many job requirements, for example, may mean that fewer women will apply because they don't meet 100 percent of them.[2] Remember that men will frequently apply for a job if they meet only 60 percent of the job qualifications. Words like "ninja" or "rock star" may also turn women off and prevent them from applying.

Similarly, be aware that when you include phrases like "fast-paced environment" or "join our tribe," it can feel exclusionary or offensive to some, in this case people with disabilities or indigenous peoples, respectively. You need to take the perspective of the underrepresented candidate pool you want to attract and make sure that you are speaking to them in a way that they can see themselves in the roles you want to hire. Do some research and try to get input from others where you can.

## 2. Source Beyond Your Usual Networks

The next step after drafting your job description is to figure out how to get a diverse pool of candidates to apply. It usually takes a lot more than putting your job description up on your website. You need to intentionally reach out beyond your usual networks and post the job to groups that are geared toward underrepresented communities. Cultivating a diverse network; asking for referrals to amazing, underrepresented talent; and spreading the word that you want a diverse set of candidates to apply will all help you attract a more diverse pipeline of applicants.

It's also important to build long-term relationships with organizations dedicated to increasing the number of people from underrepresented backgrounds in your industry. Your company must build credibility with marginalized communities for people from those communities to want to apply. Think beyond conference sponsorships and recruiting events to community efforts like volunteering and philanthropy, or more formalized partnerships designed to develop a broader pipeline of talent into your firm, such as apprenticeship or boot camp programs for underrepresented groups (URGs) that specifically train for the skills in demand for your industry.

## 3. Design a Structured and Consistent Interview Process

Let's assume you've attracted a diverse candidate pool. If you want to increase the chances of one of those candidates accepting the job, it's essential that you've clearly defined your hiring criteria and developed a structured and thoughtful interview process. I can't stress enough how defining your hiring criteria early on will help you avoid more bias later.

Gathering your interview team together before you talk to candidates and coming up with a plan on who will be focused on what kinds of skill sets and questions, as well as agreeing on what a great answer looks like versus a merely good answer, will help people evaluate candidates more consistently across the board. It will also make your interview process better in general so you'll have more confidence in your ability to hire great talent, period.

Stay focused on asking questions that are relevant to the requirements of the role. It's important that those questions are standardized for each candidate, so interviewers are not judging candidates based solely on whether or not they would want to have a beer with them afterward. To that point, make the interview team as diverse as possible so that the people you're interviewing can see themselves at your firm.

Ensure that you are accommodating people with different needs and abilities, such as asking if they need any accommodations or offering to send questions out ahead of time for candidates who might not speak fluent English or need more time to process. Often, companies look for "culture fit," which can result in "more of the same" as opposed to increasing the diversity of your teams. Instead, craft interview questions that focus on who might be a "culture add," building your culture toward the inclusive environment you want it to be.

### 4. Evaluate Candidates with Concrete Feedback

Objectivity is an important part of the evaluation process. It's a good practice for the interview team to write notes during and immediately after the interview and then assign an objective rating. You also have to be really clear about not just writing down your impressions but actually citing concrete examples of why you have those impressions.

Too often, it's only the impressions with no reasoning to back them up that get written down and read. This can lead to snap judgments based on perceptions that may come from unconscious bias. It's important to train hiring managers on how to identify bias in the interview feedback so that they can make the hiring yes or no decision more effectively and not just based on something that felt "off."

Some companies have instituted a hiring committee composed of people from diverse backgrounds who have a good track record of hiring successful candidates to the firm. The hiring committee is tasked with evaluating feedback based on consistent criteria that is not dependent on a particular function or role, which is helpful for objectivity and the ability to maintain consistency in the quality of hires across the organization.

### 5. Give Candidates a Sense of Belonging

So you've decided that you want to extend an offer to a person from an underrepresented background. How do you ensure that they accept it? It's absolutely essential that you are humble and recognize that this person has the power to choose. You must demonstrate that you have an inclusive culture and that they will feel a sense of belonging once they join the team.

Share your company's commitment to diversity, equity, inclusion, and belonging, and describe the efforts underway to support it, referring especially to any employee resource groups that people might be interested in joining. Be prepared to answer honestly any questions the candidate may have about your company's diversity numbers and opportunities to grow into leadership positions.

Offer to have them meet with others to talk about DEIB and the company's culture if they'd like to hear more directly about the experiences of people from underrepresented groups.

Highlight benefits and policies that you know are important to the candidate. If you've been intentional about being inclusive throughout your entire hiring process, it will be an easy decision for underrepresented candidates to choose you over a competitor.

Creating and executing an inclusive hiring process involves a great deal of intentionality and consistency. But the benefits of doing so far outweigh the effort involved. Focusing on inclusion will ensure that you have created a hiring process that is good for everyone, not just any one group, and it will bring in a diverse talent pool that will contribute to business success.

## Leveraging the Zeigeist

Sometimes, though, you get the opportunity to be part of the zeitgeist, and you've got to take advantage of it. This is what happened to my chief people officer colleague. She deployed her recruiting strategies and ended up hiring over a hundred people in the span of six months, which for a 200-person company was quite game changing.

But before you rush out and do what she did, it's important to recognize that their hiring success was primarily driven by only one of their strategies—the transportation hub wrap (transit billboard) campaign. Because they didn't have a huge budget, they had to be creative in how they used their resources. Instead of hiring high-priced models to put in their billboard ads, they took photos of their own employees and used their quotes on why they worked for the company.

You might suppose that the engineer with a huge following or the nose ring–wearing millennial with the colorful hair attracted the most attention, but it turned out that one of their female engineers wearing a simple T-shirt and black-rimmed glasses stole the show. With her long, dark hair and wide brown eyes set in a heart-shaped face, she was so different from the Silicon Valley techie archetype of a nerdy-ish, hoodie-wearing male that many people reacted with disbelief. The company's Twitter account blew up with comments like, "There's no way she's an engineer. She's a model." "They photoshopped her arms in which is how you can tell she's a model." And "No f**cking way she's an engineer."

The employee who was the star of that campaign was outraged that people would think that she had to look a certain way to be an engineer. So she struck back with her own hashtag campaign that happened to be one of the top 100 stories Googled that year: #ilooklikeanengineer.[3] This hashtag inspired the rest of the nonstereotypical tech world to chime in and add their own photos, tweets, and memes about how no one has to look a certain way in order to do what they love.

It was a moment of massive attention for the company. People reached out to them from universities, big press outlets, and local publications, all wanting to know who was behind this masterfully planned recruiting campaign. Even NASCAR wanted to feature the company in one of their races. The world was supporting the hashtag campaign and all that it stood for, and the company's name was being blasted into outer space, literally—NASA astronauts joined in on the fun and tweeted a photo of female scientists with the #ilooklikeanengineer hashtag.

When the campaign kicked off, the CPO didn't initially think she'd have many allies, but other executives rallied in support. Their CEO went on camera multiple times to give interviews about how he was proud of the company's employee for speaking out against anyone who questioned her engineering chops simply based on her looks. And their vice president of product was a fierce advocate for propelling more women into top executive and technical roles. With these two leading the way, the rest of the company quickly followed suit.

The CPO thought it would take longer to build a more diverse company, but the #ilooklikeanengineer campaign accelerated her ability to attract and hire highly qualified, diverse talent. Their female applicant rate doubled, and their minority applicant rate went up by 25 percent during the press cycle. In the end, this work made her realize that she wasn't alone and that the tide and appetite to change the status quo could be catalyzed by a broader movement. The recruiting campaign taught her four things about recruiting for more diversity at a company:

1.  Creative marketing plans can happen serendipitously, so take advantage of the opportunity if you become part of the zeitgeist.

2.  Stereotypes suck. No one should have to look a certain way in order to do what they love.

3.  Social media is a powerful force in shaping or destroying you or your company's brand and reputation, so use it to spread a positive message about inclusion.

4.  You have allies all around you. Sometimes you just need to start the conversation to find them.

The company enjoyed strong business success that year as well. Sometimes, when you least expect it, a simple business need, in this case a recruiting campaign, serves as a catalyst to start a dialogue around diversity that allows allies to stand up and fight for what we all know to be true: diverse teams drive better business results. It's important not to let these opportunities pass you by. You have to lean into them in order to reap the rewards.

## REDUCE BIAS IN PERFORMANCE REVIEWS

Once somebody is hired, they are expected to perform. Then typically once a year, we evaluate their performance against a set of goals—the dreaded performance review. This is another talent process that is typically rife with bias. Add to that the fact that just about everyone hates performance reviews and very few people deliver them well, it's clear that creating a more equitable performance review process is difficult.

For the most part, performance review processes are cumbersome and complex, and they add questionable value. They are, however, a necessary part of the way many companies evaluate employee performance. When companies invest in performance reviews, it's equally important to invest just as much into reducing bias throughout the process. Otherwise, we lose the opportunity to effectively develop and retain more people from underrepresented groups in leadership roles. There are three key steps necessary to de-bias performance reviews:

1. Educate everyone.

2. Run a structured process.

3. Analyze and course correct.

## 1. Educate Everyone

It's important to train your workforce in how to conduct performance evaluations effectively. This starts with understanding how different types of bias can affect performance reviews. Keep in mind, these biases also tend to affect all sorts of other decisions, including hiring and career development. But in this section, I'm going to focus on four specific types of bias that rear their ugly heads in reviews, and give you some strategies to help reduce their impact.

### Attribution Bias
When we do something well, we think it's due to our own merit: "I finished that project on time and under budget because of my superior planning and organizational skills." But when we do something badly, we think it's because of external factors, like luck or other people's mistakes: "That project went over budget because the vendor didn't ship on time and I had to scramble to get everything done." When we evaluate others, we tend to think the opposite is true: "She caught that

mistake because she got lucky." "He didn't deliver that project on time because he doesn't know how to collaborate effectively."

This catch-22 in performance feedback and evaluations can be difficult to recognize. However, managers can mitigate *attribution bias* by pausing and asking themselves if they are accurately attributing results to the person or the situation. Also, being clear about the evidence they have to support their evaluations can help clarify whether their impressions are truly reflective of the person's skills and potential. Similar to taking interview notes in hiring, sharing concrete examples are absolutely necessary in de-biasing feedback.

### Recency Bias

We tend to remember what's most recent, and that can skew our overall perceptions in a big way. Annual review processes are especially vulnerable to this *recency bias*. I can't remember what I ate for lunch yesterday, let alone something a peer did on a project a year ago. It's easier to focus on something a person did last month. But if you had a not-so-great result on that recent project but actually did a stellar job in the 11 months before that, you wouldn't want your manager to focus on only the last month, would you?

Managers and peer reviewers should make the effort to think back beyond what happened most recently and look at the cumulative set of accomplishments and opportunities to learn over time. Develop a practice to document examples of what you and your colleagues are doing well and what needs improvement as soon as it happens, so you won't have to remember it all at annual review time. Sending feedback emails to recognize great work and lessons learned after key milestones is a great way to have an online trail that you can file and look up later.

### Confirmation Bias

*Confirmation bias* refers to the tendency to search for, interpret, focus on, and remember information in a way that confirms our preconceptions: "When she showed up early to our meeting, I knew she was a good project manager." "I think he is a go-getter because I see him working out in the gym every day, just the way I do."

There are two issues with this bias. First, it means we may be excluding critical information in our evaluations because we are focusing only on validating our impressions. Second, those impressions may be based on stereotypes and therefore may not be a true reflection of that individual's accomplishments or work style.

Managers in particular need to step back and ask themselves what evidence they might have seen that runs counter to their impressions, essentially playing devil's advocate on themselves. Also, asking for input from a diverse set of colleagues in evaluations can really help a manager to get a fuller picture of the person's strengths and areas for development. Look for patterns in the feedback and include themes that can round out a picture of the person you're evaluating.

### Halo and Horns Effects

When we attach too much significance to a single thing about a person, it tends to affect our opinions of everything else about that person. This can happen in a positive way: "He is great at speaking onstage, so he must be a great leader." This is known as the *halo effect*. Or it can happen in a negative way: "She didn't show up on time, so she's probably very lazy." This the *horns effect*.

The key to reducing the impact of the halo and horns effects is to ask yourself if the evidence you are using to support your impression of a person is actually relevant. For instance, being a great public speaker isn't a real indicator of a person's leadership skills. It just means they can speak well in front of crowds. The concrete evidence you use has to be related to your assessment of the person's skills and abilities. Asking a colleague to review your evaluation can be helpful for spotting any inconsistencies like this so you can correct it.

## 2. Run a Structured Process

Reducing bias in performance management really depends on running a structured review process. Ensuring that there is documentation of clear examples of behaviors and results achieved, getting really clear on the standards for assigned ratings, gathering diverse inputs for performance, agreeing on how you're evaluating someone for promotion, and running calibration sessions where all voices are heard—all of those steps are necessary to an effective performance management system.

Do you have documented goals that you can measure employee progress against? Have you taken into account changing conditions that contributed to the results achieved? Are you evaluating each member of your team against appropriate expectations for their level and role? These are the basics. If you want to join the more advanced club, you need to focus on your calibration session design.

*Calibration sessions* can be somewhat mysterious to the uninitiated. Only people managers get invited, and oftentimes, not every people manager will actually get that opportunity. These sessions are usually run during a limited time period, which means that the people who get discussed are generally the outliers, not the majority middle. This is just a practical necessity. Otherwise, everyone would spend days discussing every single person in an organization, especially if it's really large.

The trick is ensuring that you are calibrating similar roles together and breaking down your calibration sessions by function and level. You should ensure that all directors are discussing senior managers, and senior managers are discussing managers below them, and so on. Try to review every employee, and hold shorter calibration sessions if the groups get too large for this to happen within your time frame.

Opening a calibration session with a reminder of the criteria against which you are calibrating each level, and a reminder of the different types of bias to watch out for, can help ground participants in the right mindset for the discussion.

Creating a culture where people feel free to call out bias when they see it and discuss constructive ways to mitigate it benefits more than just performance evaluations. Implementing strategies that consider all candidates who are eligible for a promotion, not just those who are nominated or put themselves forward, can be a great way to combat bias and potentially increase the number of people from underrepresented groups in leadership positions.

As described in Chapter 1, when GoDaddy executives implemented a process by which they asked managers to evaluate all candidates eligible for a promotion, not just the ones who asked, they were able to increase promotions of women by 30 percent.[4]

By being very intentional about making the process better for everyone, we can fulfill our promise of leveraging all talent, from all different backgrounds and experiences, to its fullest potential.

## 3. Analyze and Course Correct

Many companies make the mistake of not building in enough time in their performance review process to analyze their review data and course correct before ratings are finalized if there are clear patterns of bias. You have to include this step in your process to look at both the language that is used in evaluations as well as the distribution of ratings across different demographics, such as race or gender.

Studies have shown that women tend to get evaluated more negatively than men on the same behaviors and receive less constructive feedback than men do.[5] A review of language used in documented reviews can help uncover and challenge the assessments should you see this pattern emerge in your own data. It's best to do this analysis right after initial ratings are submitted and before managers go into calibration sessions. Arm your HR partners with the data and guidance on how to work with business leaders to reexamine their ratings.

I set aside time during the review cycle to coach our HR partners on how to handle these conversations and take part in calibration sessions when necessary. It's helpful to prepare your managers for this too because they will have to dig deep and be as objective as possible to determine if any changes need to be made to their initial evaluations.

Asking someone to take on the role of *Diversity Challenger* during the review process can also help uncover unintentional bias in ratings. When you designate someone during calibration sessions to take on the role of asking probing questions—calling out differences in how people with similar roles are evaluated and ensuring that underrepresented people are not overlooked—it can make your calibration more fair and equitable.

You have to make sure your Diversity Challenger (a) has the skill set to do this in a way that doesn't raise people's defenses and (b) isn't in a position where challenging might negatively affect their own review as well. Oftentimes, people look to HR to play this role, but I have found that having a high-level manager who is familiar with the team's roles but does not sit within that team's hierarchy tends to have the best outcome.

## DEVELOP THE NEXT GENERATION OF DIVERSE LEADERS

So, you've hired people from underrepresented backgrounds, and they're performing. What are you doing with this talent now that they're in the door? Are you creating an inclusive culture and environment where that diverse talent can thrive? Are you putting as much focus and as many resources into supporting them as you did to get them in? This area is the Achilles' heel of so many companies. The focus is solely on hiring, but as we saw from the Diversity Equation, if you don't spend just as much time and energy on keeping people, you're wasting your effort.

One of the top drivers of employee engagement is career growth and development.[6] We also know that the more engaged employees are at work, the more likely you are to retain them. It makes sense that companies would invest in leadership development as a way to not only grow future leaders at the company but to also improve company performance. Yet, we aren't seeing that investment translate into more underrepresented groups at the top.[7]

What should companies do to actively support and encourage people from underrepresented backgrounds into leadership roles? I believe that developing more diverse leadership at a company involves two issues. One, we want to help people from underrepresented backgrounds develop the leadership skills and confidence they need to fulfill those next-level roles. Two, we also need to ensure that those in the majority groups develop the capability to ally with and embrace the different perspectives and potential that those from underrepresented groups bring to the table. It's necessary to do both, but first, let's focus on the leadership development opportunities companies can seize upon for their underrepresented talent.

## 1. Leverage ERGs as Development Opportunities

When companies treat employee resource groups (ERGs) as volunteer organizations with a singular focus on building a community of support around a particular affinity, they are missing an opportunity. As discussed in Chapter 2, ERGs should be seen as business-related resources aligned to their strategic talent goals—one of which is to develop the next generation of leaders inside the company.

When people get involved in ERGs, it should be clear that one of the benefits of joining is the opportunity to develop new leadership skills beyond their current role. They should be given visibility to senior leaders through their ERG work. All ERGs should have executive sponsorship and involvement to support their charter. When people from underrepresented backgrounds are given opportunities to showcase their growing leadership skills through roles such as driving communications, organizing events, or educating others, they make a real impact on the business.

I've seen this approach work. When I worked at a large tech company, there was a female director in an IT role leading the women's ERG. Through her experience in the ERG, she was not only able to move the company's agenda for women forward but she also ended up making a career switch into HR, where she became a high-level HR officer at the company. Leading the ERG was one of the experiences that opened her eyes to new leadership possibilities. And she's now been at the same company for over a decade.

This is just one small example of how fully utilizing the potential of ERGs can be a massive advantage for individual employees and for the company as a whole. More and more these days, ERGs are being positioned as part of a company's leadership development pipeline, where leaders are nominated based on their future leadership potential at the company.

GE appoints its ERG leaders from the top 600 individuals identified at the company. Lockheed Martin puts ERG leaders through a leadership fundamentals program designed to groom them for other leadership roles at the company. At Bristol-Meyers Squibb, ERG leaders are full-time, dedicated roles for high performers chosen through an open and rigorous evaluation process.[8] These companies are at the forefront of recognizing how much ERG leadership roles can contribute to their succession pipeline.

## 2. Implement Targeted Leadership Development Programs

It's important to create a targeted curriculum for people from under-represented backgrounds in any foundational leadership development programs you have at your company. Why? Because different populations are dealing with very specific issues that cannot be addressed with a standard one-size-fits-all program.

It is essential that you provide a safe space to address the unique challenges that, for example, women, people of color, people with disabilities, or someone who intersects all three and more are experiencing. These specific concerns get overlooked in general leadership development programs. And by not addressing them, you are not fully supporting their leadership potential inside the company, and, in fact, you may be unwittingly putting up additional barriers to their growth.

One way I've put this into action was to develop a six-month leadership coaching program for one company's Black employees. The goal was to accelerate their career advancement by giving them the tools and support they needed to fulfill their potential, and to do it at scale with 100 employees in the first cohort. In the very first session, participants were so moved by the opportunity to discuss their shared experiences, and learn how to break through any limiting beliefs they held, that we were inundated with requests to expand the number of spots.

At the end of the program, participants reported feeling seen and invested in, and for many of them, it was the first time in their careers they had felt that way. So we expanded the program to Latinx and parent employees as well. Just knowing that they were considered leaders worth investing in made a significant difference to their sense of engagement, development, and belonging.

Wells Fargo launched its Diverse Leaders Program in 2004, targeting Asian & Pacific Islander, Black/African American, Latino, or lesbian, gay, bisexual, and transgender (LGBT) employees. Participants in this three-day program learned how to embrace their diversity dimensions as a strength to be leveraged in their leadership journey. Over 3,900 people have gone through this program so far and are more likely to stay with Wells Fargo and be promoted than non-alumni.[9] This is another important measure of success for any DEIB initiative.

## 3. Increase Mentoring and Sponsorship by Senior Leaders

A study in the *Harvard Business Review* reported on research that tracked companies' different diversity tactics and correlated them to the representation of women and racial and/or ethnic minorities in managerial roles over five years. The researchers found that mentoring programs made companies' manager ranks significantly more diverse, with up to 24 percent increases in certain demographics.[10]

It is clear that receiving good career guidance from a mentor on how to handle and navigate the political landscape inside a company makes a huge difference in the ability of those being mentored to advance. Many people in majority groups receive this guidance easily through early exposure to mentoring or existing networks. In contrast, for many in non-majority groups, it can be difficult to find a mentor when they have no internal network to draw on or any idea of how to go about it.

And because mentoring can lead to sponsorship by those mentors, it's important for underrepresented individuals to build those relationships. For many, this will require companies to create formal mentoring and sponsor programs to match underrepresented talent to senior leaders at the company. This can be an opportunity for the learning to go both ways. URGs can increase leadership's understanding of their lived experiences as a reverse mentor, and leaders can increase URGs' understanding of how to succeed in their companies.

Once a mentor becomes strongly invested in their mentee's success, then you've created a sponsor. This can either happen through a formalized expectation or more organically as a mentee earns a sponsor's support over time. Sponsors matter because they will advocate for you when you are not in the room. They will be the ones at decision-making tables to convince others that you deserve to advance into that next-level leadership role. For example, in studies conducted by David Smith, associate professor at the U.S. Naval War College, and Brad Johnson, psychology professor at the United States Naval Academy (USNA), researchers found that when women are sponsored by men, they make more money, get more promotions, and have better career outcomes.[11]

I have personally been a beneficiary of many mentors and their eventual sponsorship over the years. One mentor hired me into my first diversity and inclusion program role. Another mentor advocated for me when I was seeking a promotion midcareer. After becoming an independent consultant, yet another mentor referred me to companies that needed additional expertise and perspective on their diversity and inclusion strategies. I am just one example of many that show how active mentoring and sponsorship can lead to amazing tangible outcomes.

## 4. Build Allyship

We need to expand our thinking of what leadership looks like and actively include people with different leadership styles, untraditional backgrounds, and different life experiences. Leveraging programs to accelerate the leadership development of underrepresented talent will help us democratize opportunity and change the face of leadership today to be more diverse and inclusive.

But these strategies won't work on their own. They need to be coupled with strategies to disrupt bias and existing perceptions that those in decision-making positions may hold about who advances and who does not. It's not about teaching people who are different how to conform to the norm. It's about teaching people who make up the norm to redefine what the norm is.

This means that in every leadership development program you deliver at your company, you need to do two things.

First, you should incorporate bias and inclusive leadership concepts into the curriculum and embed an understanding of what it means to be an ally and upstander within that. This kind of training can run in parallel with the curriculum that you develop specific to URG groups. You can also roll these kinds of trainings out more broadly as part of your overarching learning and development (L&D) mandate to support an inclusive environment, as long as you ensure that your leadership participates as well.

Second, just as we talked about with hiring and performance reviews, you need to ensure that you have a structured process for determining who gets to participate in these kinds of programs and be very intentional about ensuring an equitable process around that. For instance, many leadership programs are targeted by job level, like directors or VPs. Unfortunately, given the low numbers of URGs at those levels within a company, you may find it to be extremely difficult to have more than a handful of Black or Latinx people participating in any single cohort in the program. Which means you may have to plan on going deeper into the organization, to a level below director, to find more high-potential URG candidates to tap for these programs.

There's also the issue of nominations versus applications to participate in these programs. Both have inherent bias built in. If you use a nomination process, managers usually go with the most visible or top-of-mind people, which can disadvantage groups that don't fit the existing leadership mold. But if you use an application process, you need to understand that many people from URGs suffer from imposter syndrome, which can mean they don't feel they have what it takes to be a leader at the company and therefore don't apply.

So I always advocate for a combination of both. Everyone with the right level of experience and title should be eligible for nomination, not just those who have expressed a desire to advance. And ask managers to have a conversation with employees who are part of a URG about their potential to be in the program and encourage them to apply.

Everyone has a role to play in supporting a diverse and inclusive environment in the workplace. Corporate cultures are an embodiment of all the experiences each person has within your company. And since no person is an island, people from underrepresented groups must interact with people who are different from them most of the time that they are at work. Which means those in the majority need to do the really heavy lifting to create an inclusive environment that is free of barriers to opportunity, treats everyone with respect, and makes space for those who are not like themselves.

## PUTTING IT INTO ACTION

Pick a talent process: hiring, performance review, or leadership development.

Pull together a working group of key stakeholders, especially representatives from URGs.

As a group, map out each step in the process you've chosen, and discuss these questions:

1. Is our process really getting us the results we want to see?

2. Where can potential bias creep in at each step?

3. Who is falling out of the process, and at which step?

4. Have we gotten input from URGs on their experiences of the process?

5. What have we not tried yet in our efforts to improve this process?

Brainstorm potential solutions to prototype.

Test those solutions on a small scale to see what adjustments need to be made if any.

Implement and continue to iterate for improvement.

# MORE THAN TRAINING

When I was consulting, the most frequent request I received from potential clients was to come in and do unconscious bias training for employees. I would always be happy to do this, but my first question to these clients was, "What is your overall DEIB strategy, and how does this bias training fit into that?" Nine times out of 10, companies would tell me they had no clear strategy. Then they would tell me that their employees had been asking them to do more on DEIB, and the leaders felt that starting with training was the best answer to give.

This is a very common scenario. In fact, every time I started a new in-house role, the demand for training was the first request on the table. Usually, before strategy, before recruiting, even before bringing a leader like me on board, DEIB training has been the go-to tactic to help companies feel like they are doing something tangible in support of an inclusive culture.

Don't get me wrong, I believe that DEIB training plays a necessary role in getting everyone at a company on the same baseline foundation level of knowledge about the issues in this space, and it can drive insightful experiences for individuals, which then motivates them to engage in different actions. However, too often it's used as a crutch for when companies don't know what else to do or how else to tackle the problems. And when training isn't connected to any kind of strategy, it can backfire.

There is a significant body of research that says that unconscious bias training is not effective.[12] There can be multiple reasons for this.

When diversity training is mandatory, employees can resent that. People do not like to be told what to do or how to think. No one wants to be treated as if they are in a remedial course to correct for bad behaviors. And very often, diversity training is rolled out in response to bad behaviors, which is not lost on many employees who will then show up angry and not be open to learning. Those folks can derail the learning for everyone else in the class.

Sometimes, the content of diversity training can be perceived as blaming white, straight men for all the bias, prejudice, and discrimination that minoritized groups experience. When this happens, it sets up an us-versus-them dynamic that does not motivate the inclusive leadership behaviors we want. Lastly, there are studies that show emphasizing the value of diversity and suppressing stereotypes can spark more biased behaviors rather than less because people tend to remember the stereotypes discussed rather than the lessons they are supposed to be learning in the course.[13] There's also the risk of complacency when you perceive your company to be a "nondiscriminatory" environment. You're less likely to view your own biased behavior as biased.[14]

With all of this evidence saying diversity training doesn't work, why then do a majority of companies do it? Some do it because they don't know what else to do. Others believe and hope they are doing it differently enough to be effective. Still others believe that doing something is better than doing nothing and implementing training is one of the quickest, easiest, and most visible actions a company can take to support DEIB. It can also protect companies from discrimination lawsuits as they can point to their training rollout as evidence they care about DEIB.

Ultimately, we incorrectly assume that mere education and awareness of the issues can help us better address them. But they are effective only if we do them correctly. To do this successfully, research shows that you cannot implement diversity training in isolation and expect it to reduce bias in the workplace on its own.[15]

It must be part of a broader strategy made up of multiple, complementary components that address DEIB issues holistically. These components can include things like targeted college recruitment programs, formal mentoring and sponsorship programs, diversity task forces with accountability to drive solutions, and management training programs delivered by managers themselves. These all work to give company leaders closer proximity to people who are different from themselves, thus exposing them to the issues experienced by minoritized groups in ways that can turn them into champions of diversity.

The other problem I often see is that training is done as a one-off event. Company leaders rush to conduct training in response to external events. A prime example of this happened back in 2018, when Starbucks closed all 8,000 of its US stores for half a day to conduct racial equity training among its 175,000 employees.[16] This was in response to an incident at a Philadelphia Starbucks where two Black men who were waiting for a friend were arrested for not purchasing anything. The backlash was immediate as many people sit in a Starbucks without purchasing anything and are not arrested. Seen as an instance of racial bias, Starbucks reacted swiftly with an apology and response, with promises for more ongoing training and dialogue in the future. The company acknowledged that one four-hour workshop was not going to undo decades of learned conditioning or our basic human tendency to be positively biased toward in-groups and negatively biased toward out-groups. But it was a start.

Yet, too many companies invest in diversity training as if it is something that will solve all their diversity problems once it's done, and often they don't plan for how to continue reinforcing the education in the long term. You have to be realistic about what training can actually accomplish. It won't move the needle on your hiring of underrepresented groups, or decrease the number of racially charged employee relations issue reports, or drive long-term changes in behaviors if you're exposing people to only a single workshop every two years. I'm not sure any one-time training can do that.

Developing a road map of offerings that build on each other over time is helpful to keep the learning ongoing. I usually partner with in-house learning and development experts to assess our learning needs and come up with a sequence of topics, session formats, and delivery methods to ensure that we offer education for everyone from beginners to people who are already knowledgeable in the space.

## Applying CARE to Training

Part of any good approach to effective DEIB training is to design it with CARE in mind. I don't mean just teaching CARE as part of the curriculum but really integrating it into your program.

One case study of how to do this comes from a chief diversity officer at a consumer goods company. He wanted to provide DEI training that would have a significant impact. He saw this as an integral step to help the company become more inclusive and welcoming. He knew that unconscious bias training had had mixed success, so he consciously avoided calling it "training" and created the content working with consultants and internal stakeholders. The curriculum focused on five objectives:

1. Raise awareness of marginalized lived experiences.

2. Increase understanding of bias and its impact.

3. Own our bias.

4. Apply tools to mitigate bias.

5. Commit to being more inclusive.

Their first goal was to raise awareness of what it is like to be a person of color, particularly a Black person, in the United States. This curriculum was on the heels of George Floyd's murder in 2020, and the initial focus was on the challenges of Black Americans.

The two-hour sessions are carefully facilitated and involve groups of 25 to 35 individuals via videoconference. They raise awareness of issues by sharing a powerful, nine-minute video providing firsthand accounts of what it's like to leave your house as a Black person. It discusses the challenge of being profiled and followed around in stores; being singled out to show an ID when using a credit card at a store; being asked if "you are paying for items with SNAP" (formerly known as "food stamps"), when you had no intention of doing so, at a grocery store in communities where you are clearly a minority; and so forth. This is followed by real-life stories of fellow employees who have been victims of bias. These stories help employees who haven't experienced these situations to walk in other people's shoes.

Not only did the training require *courage* from employees to share their stories, it also required courage from participants to share their honest reactions when facilitators asked participants to respond to what was discussed. How did they feel? What were the key takeaways? Conversations often are raw and emotional, as people tell stories about being raised in environments such as South Africa under apartheid that were anything but welcoming for people of color. It took a lot of trust for employees to open up and be vulnerable in sharing their personal stories and insights. Participants described sessions as "eye-opening," and remarks such as, "Now, as a white person, I realize that invisible doors have been open to me that weren't open to others" were common to hear.

They soon added discussion points and scenarios about other ethnic groups, women, and LGBTQ+ individuals. This included the opportunity for women to "school the men" about what it's like to be a woman in corporate America. They shared stories about being repeatedly talked over or disregarded in meetings, being overlooked for promotions because of preconceived notions about the role of women at work, and more. One particularly memorable story involved a business trip, before joining the company, where the men wanted to go to a strip club and invited their female coworkers to join them. This completely unacceptable activity highlighted how much education was needed.

With a raised awareness of what it's like to be a person of color, additional stories of people of color being treated unfairly because of bias are shared to address the second objective of increasing understanding of bias and its impact. Attendees are asked to imagine, if they were there when the poor treatment occurred, what would they have said or done? For example, would they have intervened and asked the store clerk or other individual displaying bias why they treated the person of color that way? Facilitators ask if attendees would have felt able to affirm the person of color by saying, "I saw what happened, and it was wrong. I'm so sorry that happened. I support you." The attendees then take a moment to discuss how important that could have been to the situation. The purpose is to *empower* participants to become allies—not to put themselves in harm's way, but to be more willing to say something if they see injustice unfolding in front of them.

Sometimes, the facilitator will mention Martin Luther King, Jr.'s quote: "In the end, we won't remember the words of our enemies. We'll remember the silence of our friends." Other participants have added, "Sometimes to say nothing [when you see wrongdoing] is like saying something."

For the third objective to own our bias, the content addresses the fact that about 99.9 percent of us have some form of bias. Many people don't want to acknowledge it, but the goal is for these conversations to be authentic and *respectful* of different lived experiences. And to acknowledge the reality that essentially everyone is predisposed to feel some sort of bias for or against one or more groups or types of people. It doesn't mean we are all bad people. It just means that we have to recognize how bias can affect how we view and treat others and be open to doing something about it.

To achieve their fourth goal, tools that can help identify and combat one's bias are highlighted. This involves elements such as slowing down to reflect on why an individual feels the way they do about a certain individual or group. It also involves exercising empathy, by trying to put yourself in the shoes of others you may feel biased against. Another element of empathy is the active willingness to learn more about people who are different from you. What's their story? How do they see the world? And once you're open to learning more about others, you can start finding positive examples about groups that individuals are more distant from or even biased against. Doing this can help pave the way toward less bias toward that group.

Now that participants have the tools to support their DEIB journey, each session ends with *accountability* to reinforce the fifth objective by asking all participants to think about and then commit to one thing they're willing to do to be more inclusive. Facilitators underscore that it's not about giving a recommendation to others. It's about what they're willing to do personally and what they will hold themselves accountable to. For many, this is the most impactful part of the sessions, when individuals can think about their own goals but also get ideas from and be inspired by others.

The company was also thoughtful about how it rolled out the training. They launched a couple of pilot sessions to test and tweak the content and held extensive train-the-trainer sessions with the facilitators. In less than a year, several thousand of the company's top leaders experienced the curriculum. Another 3,000 were scheduled to experience it later in the year.

A critical contributor to the company's successful rollout was its senior managers' support for these efforts in both words and actions. They committed early on, and their commitment buoyed the training effort tremendously. They received hundreds of unsolicited, positive responses to their program from individuals' perspectives on bias and suggestions as to how they could move forward in positive ways. The company experienced from 10 to 20 percent increases in just a year's time in a number of key metrics involving promotions of women and people of color. More importantly, they formed a team of committed leaders focused on positive change and ongoing learning. Employees wanted to learn more about how they could support these efforts, and employee resource group involvement nearly doubled.

To extend the learning, the company also shared the Harvard Implicit Association Test as one way individuals could learn more about the types of bias they may have.[17] And they launched a monthly inclusion series, with modules that typically took less than 10 minutes to complete, in addition to other opportunities to engage in courageous conversations. All of this was done with a focus on helping individuals continually learn and grow to become the best version of themselves.

From this process, it's clear that applying the principles of courage, accountability, respect, and empowerment (CARE) to training can be incredibly impactful. Storytelling and active interaction are more powerful than the standard lecture or presentation approach. And leading with a genuine goal to try to help people can change hearts and minds.

## PUTTING IT INTO ACTION

Using the template in Table 4.1, list the different audiences you want to train:

- What are your learning objectives for each audience?

- What topics are most important to teach?

- Include format, owner-facilitator, and timing.

### Table 4.1 Training Plan

| Audience | Topic | Learning Objectives | Learning Format | Owner-Facilitator | Timing |
|---|---|---|---|---|---|
|  |  |  |  |  |  |
|  |  |  |  |  |  |
|  |  |  |  |  |  |
|  |  |  |  |  |  |

## KEY TAKEAWAYS

1. *Inclusive hiring* means looking at your hiring process end to end, developing strategies to not only attract more diverse talent to your company but also to remove unintentional barriers to hiring them.

2. Performance reviews are often the most difficult process in which to mitigate bias. Educate yourself on the many different kinds of biases that can affect your perception of a person's performance, and actively work to minimize their effects.

3. Leadership development is just as much about developing allies who can recognize and value the qualities that URGs bring into leadership as it is about helping URGs develop their own, authentic leadership to advance.

4. For any kind of DEIB training to successfully support change, it must be tied to a bigger strategy and provide ongoing skill building and reinforcement.

5. If you integrate CARE principles into your talent strategies and training, you are more likely to see positive results.

# CHAPTER 5

# The Importance of Community

When I got my first DEIB job, I was part of a team of two people. When I transitioned to my next role, it was just me for a few years plus an intern here and there before I got a team under me. And the next role after that was another one where I was the only DEIB person at the company. It was apparent to me early on that I needed to find my community of DEIB professionals so I wouldn't feel isolated as the only person in this function at those companies.

I decided to reach out to various DEIB professionals I knew, respected, and just plain wanted to hang out with, bringing them together on a quarterly basis to share challenges, failures, and successes. It was a community of peers I trusted to commiserate with me when I was having a tough time, celebrate with me when I achieved a big milestone, and work on new ideas with me as we sought to improve DEIB together in our industry.

This is a stark example of how important it is, when you feel isolated, as so many people who are underrepresented inside companies are, to find a community of people who will support you and help you feel like you belong. This is why employee resource groups and allyship are so important. While we've mentioned them previously, this chapter expands on some key details you should consider as you launch these initiatives inside your company.

## TRANSFORM YOUR EMPLOYEE RESOURCE GROUPS

Forming employee resource groups is probably the most common way to support underrepresented groups and build community inside your company. These groups provide a safe space for marginalized people to share their experiences and seek support for whatever they might need. They are also wonderful ways to support career development for those who get involved in leadership roles and do things outside their normal day-to-day job responsibilities. However, they aren't as often leveraged in driving business initiatives or partnering with external organizations for recruiting purposes.

Earlier in my career, I helped launch a company's very first set of employee resource groups (ERGs). The ERG charters were based primarily on providing a supportive community for people from underrepresented backgrounds. As a result, their activities were focused on supporting external community organizations, professional development for members, and education to the broader company on what their cultures and issues were.

And it was great! There were volunteer events for great nonprofits, inspiring speakers came in to talk about their leadership journeys, and we had a Diversity Day celebration where each ERG showcased their culture, challenges, or history. Our employees' ratings on their sense of inclusion in our employee survey went up, and it felt like a huge success. But it actually wasn't. We were doing a great job at bringing people together, but we weren't moving the needle on our hard metrics around representation. In addition, the momentum of each ERG was hard to maintain over time with changes in ERG leadership and the expectation that this was "volunteer" work. So their real business impact was questionable.

Fast-forward to another company and one of the hardest-driving businesspeople I've ever had the good fortune to work with. She was my direct manager and, from her, I learned how to be a business leader, not just a diversity leader, because she looked at everything not through the lens of "what can I do with what I have" but instead through "what needs to be done and what will it take to get there." And she saw that the ERGs we had inherited were operating pretty much the way I described in the preceding paragraphs, and in her mind, it meant they were not relevant to the business.

So I had to turn the situation around or risk the ERGs being defunded, and that possibility drove me to a whole new way of treating ERGs, shifting them from a focus on the employee to a focus on the business. For example, instead of giving each ERG a set allocation of budget for activities each year, I implemented a strategic planning process whereby each ERG had to build a proposal for what they wanted to accomplish that was aligned with our business priorities and a business case for what resources they needed to do it.

We treated them like a business unit, where they were accountable to metrics and quarterly operating reviews. We asked ERG members to have a direct conversation with their managers to include their ERG efforts as part of their development plan so it wasn't seen as volunteer work. And our operating principle was that great ideas that further the business will get funded. If HR didn't have the resources to implement a great idea, we would find someone in the business who did. And this was all new to them and many of my peers, who were used to ERGs being positioned as volunteer groups.

Treating these ERGs more like *business resource groups* made a huge difference in terms of hiring and retaining more people from underrepresented groups, creating visibility and executive buy-in, and building professional development skills in a concrete, business-applicable way. It was because of this approach that our women's ERG drove a global career development event in which thousands of women participated and a technical recruiting event that attracted over 400 people and resulted in hires. It's amazing what ERGs can accomplish when you challenge them in the right way, give them the appropriate resources to do their work, and support them with recognition of the impact they are having.

Common questions I get from companies just starting out on their ERG journey are, what guidelines should ERGs follow, and how should they operate? Let's review some typical components of ERG guidelines you'll have to define for your ERGs to help minimize confusion and maximize their effectiveness.

## Connect ERGs to Your Business

Start off with defining why ERGs are important to your company's DEIB strategy. A sample introduction might be this:

> At Company X, respecting and encouraging diversity, equity, inclusion, and belonging (DEIB) isn't just part of who we are. It's how we succeed in today's competitive marketplace. Leveraging our employees' diverse talents to their fullest is imperative to innovating and meeting our customer needs. One of the ways we support DEI is through *employee resource groups* (ERGs). This initiative is designed to engage our employee communities more effectively to support a winning organization.

## Define What an ERG Is

Many people who haven't experienced an ERG before have no idea what it is: a company-recognized group of employees who share a common interest and engage in activities that support the company's values, culture, and business goals. Employee resource groups are driven by passionate people who want to create cross-functional communities in which employees have an opportunity to foster new business ideas, provide professional development opportunities, and champion DEIB-related issues.

ERGs can differ from informal social groups or clubs in some important ways:

1. The primary focus is not to create recreational experiences for employees but to support business goals.

2. Activities are aligned to DEIB strategies.

3. ERGs have executive sponsorship.

4. ERGs receive funding and support from HR.

It's up to you to define what makes sense for your company culture.

## Who Gets to Be a Member

I think it's particularly important to allow anyone to join any ERG. They should be open to all regardless of whether a person shares an affinity for the group or is an ally. Some might argue that ERGs should be safe spaces only for those who share an affinity to discuss issues and concerns freely. However, I think ERGs can balance both needs by being open to all and having activities that anyone can participate in, but also creating spaces that are meant solely for those who share the ERG affinity to participate in as well.

For instance, a military veterans ERG might host events like a Veterans Day recognition that are open to everyone at the company to participate in to learn about military culture. But they may also have safe community space meetings that are open only to those who have served in the military to talk about how some of them may be dealing with post-traumatic stress disorder (PTSD) and their need for mental health support.

Participating in an ERG is an opt-in process. If people take on ERG leadership roles, they should coordinate with their manager to ensure that their work is recognized and part of their performance development plan.

## Benefits of Participating

Everyone should be encouraged to get involved with ERGs. There are multiple benefits to participating, especially for those who take on leadership roles:

- Learn about diverse community issues and concerns.

- Build your skill sets in leadership or areas outside your job.

- Become part of a supportive community and network with other employees.

- Gain exposure to the senior executives who sponsor and mentor the ERGs.

- Contribute your perspective to the company's products and processes.

- Strengthen your company's ties to external underrepresented community organizations through ERG work.

## Funding

ERGs cannot operate without some form of funding from the company. Many companies allocate an amount per ERG annually, either based on membership or equitable division of their overall budget. I advocate for having a set annual budget for all ERG activities but no set allocation for each group. Each ERG is expected to submit an annual plan with proposed activities and expenses for approval. Proposals that are best aligned with DEI strategies and have the biggest opportunity for meaningful impact can then be prioritized for funding. Appropriate expenses should fall within these guidelines:

- Be related to launching the group or chapters

- Support the group's operations, infrastructure, or membership numbers

- Benefit a majority of group members

- Tie directly back to the group's goals and strategic plans

- Support the company's customer or talent objectives

It is just as important to define what ERG activities the company will *not* endorse or fund, such as the following:

- Driving agendas or objectives inconsistent with company values and policies as outlined in the company's code of ethics, equal employment opportunity policies, and/or prohibition of harassment policies

- Opposing other chartered groups

- Negotiating or dealing with the company on compensation

## Roles and Responsibilities

I've also found it helpful to define job descriptions for the different ERG roles your company might have. It gives people a good idea of expectations and sets up your ERG for better success in the future when people know what is in and out of scope for their roles and how ERG governance works. Some sample responsibilities you can expand on follow:

### ERG Leaders

- Develop and implement goals and activities of the ERG.

- Meet with all group leaders once a quarter to share best practices, support each other, and coordinate activities.

- Engage in strategic planning at the beginning of each fiscal year and communicate to HR.

### ERG Program Managers

- Provide infrastructure, funding, and support for all ERGs.

- Coordinate cross-group leadership meetings.

- Maintain an ERG advisory council.

### Executive Sponsors

- Provide advice and guidance to ERG leadership.

- Champion and publicize the ERG.

- Support and participate in ERG activities.

### ERG Advisory Councils

- Consist of members from HR, community affairs, marketing and PR, policy, government relations, and executive sponsors.

- Approve, advise, and counsel groups.

## Executive Sponsorship

It's important for ERGs to have visibility and championship at the executive level; hence, executive sponsorship is a must in my opinion. I usually ask ERG leaders to consult with me before approaching a potential executive sponsor so I can provide guidance and ensure that it will be a good match. In my experience, the most successful executive sponsors meet the following criteria:

- Have a passion for supporting diversity and inclusion

- Are recognized leaders at the company (typically VP and above)

- Believe that growing and developing talent are key priorities and competencies

- Have the bandwidth and resources available to participate in and sponsor activities of the group

- May or may not share affinity with the group, but have a desire to champion its charter

- Have a role strategically aligned with the goals of the group

## Launching an ERG

Establishing and launching an employee resource group must be supported and approved by some centralized decision maker at the company, whether it is the head of DEIB or a broader diversity council. Following is an outline of the general steps employees can take in establishing an ERG:

1. Define the group.

    a. Recruit a core leadership team with clear roles.

    b. Define group goals, ensuring alignment with business priorities.

    c. Create its organizational structure and governance process.

    d. Develop a plan of activities for the first year.

2. Gain support.

    a. Connect with the ERG program manager (if you have one) to refine initial ideas.

    b. Identify and approach an executive sponsor.

    c. Develop and submit a proposal to the ERG advisory council for approval.

3. Go public.

    a. Once approved, develop a communication plan.

    b. Partner with the appropriate channels to publicize the group:

        (1) Employee communications

        (2) New hire orientation

        (3) Talent acquisition

    c. Plan for a launch event, if appropriate.

4. Create momentum.

    a. Follow up the launch with planned activities.

    b. Recruit membership at different sites or virtually.

    c. Support the formation of other chapters.

5. Set goals annually.

    a. Once the group is established, submit the annual strategic plan to the ERG program manager for funding.

b. Review goals, org structure, and activities on a quarterly basis, and adjust as necessary.

## Operating Model

There are many different kinds of operating models for ERGs, and what works best for you will depend on your company's culture, size, locations, and governance structures. I have found that to share the burden of responsibilities, a cochair and committee structure works well to prevent burnout and loss of momentum when turnover happens. Some ERG operating guidelines are below:

### Leadership

- There is a cochair structure with a steering committee consisting of the following:
  - Leaders for major functions, such as communications, membership, finance, and programs
  - Leaders for major site locations if applicable

### Activities

- These are focused and clearly aligned with the group's overarching goals. Target activities by identifying the interests of ERG members. Here are some example activities:
  - Sponsoring a company presence at a recruiting conference
  - Organizing fundraising or donations for an affiliated nonprofit
  - Creating learning events on related topics
  - Providing feedback for internal product development or marketing campaigns

- Activities should be designed with a clear objective and identified goals. Their success could be measured through surveys, attendance, or feedback, among other relevant metrics.

- Senior leaders in the company should be involved in activities. Let them know what you are doing, and have them participate in some way to amplify impact.

- Drive effective communications around the activity and its purpose. Publicity is a way to educate people about the network.

### Meetings

- ERGs should meet regularly and as frequently as necessary for progress. Be realistic about how often you can meet.

### Facilities

- Any ERG activities taking place on company property must comply with established facilities and workplace policies and guidelines.

## Recognizing ERG Contributions

Lastly, after all the hard work that ERGs have put into supporting more DEIB at the company, you have to reward and recognize them somehow. Ensure that hourly employees have paid time to participate in ERG activities. Look at your ERG leadership pool when thinking about succession planning on your teams. Incorporate ERG work into formal performance review templates, asking how employees contributed to the culture of inclusion at your firm.

Bring ERG leaders together at least once a year for leadership development. Set up bonus or other recognition opportunities for work done specific to ERGs or championing inclusion inside your company. If DEIB is truly a company priority, then you should give people the time and rewards necessary to reflect the value their work brings to this effort.

## PUTTING IT INTO ACTION

Using Table 5.1 for a template, outline a strategic plan for an ERG at your company:

- What is the ERG's mission?

- What problem is the ERG solving for?

- List top three ERG strategic objectives for the year.

- How do they align to DEI objectives?

- How will they measure success for each objective?

- What actions will they take to support each objective?

- What resources do you need? Are there any dependencies?

- What is the timing?

Table 5.1  **ERG Charter and Strategic Plan**

| ERG mission: | | | | | |
|---|---|---|---|---|---|
| **Problem** | **Objective** | **Activity** | **Timing** | **Success Measures** | **Budget and Resources** |
| **People** | | | | | |
| | | | | | |
| | | | | | |

| Problem | Objective | Activity | Timing | Success Measures | Budget and Resources |
|---------|-----------|----------|--------|------------------|----------------------|
| Place |  |  |  |  |  |
|  |  |  |  |  |  |
| Product |  |  |  |  |  |
|  |  |  |  |  |  |
| Community |  |  |  |  |  |
|  |  |  |  |  |  |

## WE NEED MORE ALLIES

Allyship is another strong way to build community and support for DEIB. A fellow DEIB expert at a global transportation services company shared her story with me on the importance of allyship in her work. Let's call her Nancy to maintain her confidentiality. It was the fall of 2019, and she was starting to look toward the following year. Her organization had launched two new employee resource groups—LGBTQ+ and Latinx—that year already and were about to soft launch yet another group at an end-of-year celebration. With these new ERGs in place, it felt like 2020 would be a year in which they would capitalize on their momentum and dig in, introducing new initiatives.

As she began thinking about how to simplify their strategic priorities, she started picking up some cues from comments she'd heard: "Our ERG wanted to do the celebration first. It was our idea." Or, "We don't have enough large spaces in the office, and that ERG is holding several dates and times for their events." Such were the growing pains of now having three ERGs and the potential competition of even more launching in the future. It was evident that while it was good to have more ERGs, there was already a jockeying of positions to hold as much of the limited resources of airtime, physical space, and engagement of their employees as possible.

When she contemplated how to rally others around the ERGs' new events and initiatives, the light bulb went off. She needed an initiative that was relatable and approachable but would also drive change, and she settled on defining an Allyship Initiative with three objectives:

- To build trust and connection

- To build awareness of everyday actions to create momentum beyond words

- To elevate inclusive culture

Up to this point, the term *allyship* was used loosely inside the company with no connection to their DEIB goals or helping folks build their awareness and understanding. With this in mind, she set out to gain alignment around different roles employees could take within the Allyship Initiative as a first step.

## Defining Ally Roles

While it's natural for different employee resource groups to ally with each other, it's still necessary to build allyship skills among the majority so that their work is embraced and valued. Allies are people who understand the privileges they have and use that privilege to take action to support and protect those without the same privileges. You can be an ally to different communities in different ways, even if you're in an underrepresented group. For instance, I am a person of color, but I am also privileged in that I am able-bodied, and so I do my best to advocate for people with disabilities.

Anyone can call themselves an "ally," but it's really only your actions that determine whether you truly are an ally or not. Do you stand up and speak out in support of marginalized communities? Do you create space for minoritized voices to be at the table and speak their truth? Or do you let inappropriate jokes about women or other historically underrepresented groups go unchallenged when you hear them? If you do the latter and not the former, then you're not really practicing allyship.

Allyship requires you to leverage the power and privilege that you have in support of someone who has less of those things. And if you choose to sit on the sidelines and allow racial slurs or microaggressions to happen right in front of you because you don't know how to intervene or don't think it will make a difference, you're not an ally. You're just a bystander.

There's also a growing perspective that allyship is not enough to help us solve the systemic issues that continue to roadblock the advancement of underrepresented talent. A term closely associated with allyship is *accomplices*—that is, people who are taking active actions to dismantle the structures and systems holding marginalized communities back and who are willing to face the potential negative consequences for doing so. Allies work within the existing system of power to support less privileged communities. Accomplices work to deconstruct those systems and build more equitable ones in their place. In my perspective, you can be an ally without being an accomplice, but you cannot be an accomplice without being an ally, so I'll be using *allyship* as a broader, umbrella term for those who wish to actively support DEIB. However, I do believe having both allies and accomplices are necessary to advance DEIB. Nothing changes without openly challenging the uncomfortable, and individuals need to assess for themselves how much they are willing and able to risk within different contexts.

Defining what allyship means to your company is a key element to aligning everyone around it. With the Allyship Initiative mentioned earlier, Nancy developed key messaging around what allyship was about and why it was important. Once the key messages were set, she reviewed potential ally roles and determined which ones would resonate inside her company. She wanted roles that were supportive of the company's inclusion journey, were approachable, and were not difficult to model. She selected four roles, informed by Karen Catlin's work in *Better Allies*:

- *Sponsor:* Supports the work of historically minoritized colleagues, primarily in ways that will help advance those colleagues' career or brand in the workplace.

- *Amplifier:* Augments and elevates voices from marginalized communities by giving them credit, making space for them to speak, or enforcing equitable communication norms.

- *Upstander:* Not a bystander. This person sees harmful behavior and actively fights against it by intervening when someone is behaving in an offensive or prejudiced manner.

- *Confidant:* Holds safe space for people from underrepresented groups to share their perceptions, frustrations, and feelings by listening and trusting in their experiences as valid. [1]

With the ally roles identified, it was time to begin working on examples aligned to behaviors or ways of working within the company. She developed allyship examples centered around the company's core values, which most employees could recite by heart. The core values are deeply connected to her company's culture so it was essential to connect allyship with that culture. By showing up as allies, everyone could reinforce and uplift the company's values, boldly proclaiming their company's commitment to DEIB.

## Let Allyship Lead the Way

With the connection to the company's core values and culture established, Nancy then set out to link allyship with core competencies and the leadership framework. The company had already defined the expected behaviors of all employees, and it was important for leaders of the company to show that allyship was already embedded in those expectations and not only the sole responsibility of its leaders. Connecting to these two frameworks showed people that they were already acting in some capacity as allies, and they were encouraged to do even more of it, more visibly.

After this foundation was set, Nancy shared the Allyship Initiative with the company's ERGs for them to integrate it into their 2020 plans. She asked the ERGs to have at least two shared goals with other ERGs in the spirit of allyship. Shared goals were meant to build trust and connection and help address the competition and jockeying-for-airtime issue. Because the ERGs had to submit their annual plans to her at the beginning of 2020, it meant that they had to work together to identify their activities, events, or focus areas early on.

As 2020 began, she introduced their allyship focus at a large employee meeting. A new Black and African-American ERG launched in February, and other ERGs rallied around the launch and were active amplifiers. For Women's History Month in March, all the ERGs supported the women's group and celebrated underrepresented women in history. The Allyship Initiative was gaining momentum, and Nancy began to get ready to roll out their campaign on allyship companywide.

But then COVID-19 hit. Like many other organizations, the company sent everyone home. Employees had to get used to working from home and being on constant video calls. The company had to make serious, employee-impacting decisions to weather the economic downturn. It was overwhelming, and with so many changes, they had to put the Allyship Initiative on hold.

## Navigating Setbacks

Launching allyship programs can be tricky. Oftentimes, allyship programs are perceived as being based in guilt. "As a straight, white male who has more privilege than anybody else, you have a responsibility to help those less fortunate than yourself."

And while being an ally can be based in a sense of responsibility to drive a more equitable world, it is not about being blamed. I'm not here to shame you into supporting marginalized communities. But I am here to help educate you about the issues so that you can understand the extent of the problem and realize that those in underrepresented groups cannot fix it on their own. We need you to play a part, especially when times get tough.

When the murder of George Floyd spurred a global social justice movement in its aftermath, it left many people asking, "What can I do?" There was a growing intensity to address this at work, and Nancy knew she had to create a space where employees could come together and support one another. And to have options for open dialogues with a theme or call to action. So as part of her Allyship Initiative, she started Allyship Dialogues to learn, listen, discuss, exchange ideas and experiences, and explore what people could do as an ally in a safe space.

The Allyship Dialogues were 90 minutes in length, and participants dug into each of the ally roles and gave each other ideas for what to do in varying situations. Nancy emphasized that the Allyship Dialogue was to help folks build their familiarity and understanding so that they would have something to draw upon and could take action as an ally. The primary objective was to listen and learn and not allow people to say they were allies while doing nothing different. Everyone was encouraged to take action.

The first five Allyship Dialogues filled to capacity, so Nancy added more over time. Some leaders requested intact team sessions. Others wanted to help facilitate. The sessions had struck a chord with employees by providing a space to talk, share, and learn. Some folks felt the company was sending a strong message on the expectations of everyone with the sessions. By the end of 2020, they had facilitated about 25 sessions in the United States alone. They have since expanded the Allyship Dialogues to India, Latin America, and Europe, customizing the format to be relevant for each region.

Where are they today? They now have an executive sponsor for the Allyship Initiative, a vice president who understands his privilege and uses it to support and amplify those who don't have the same privilege. Allyship has made its way onto leaders' priority lists as a key way of working. ERGs continue to have allyship goals with one another as part of their yearly plans. The ERGs have also influenced their executive sponsors to be visible allies to other ERGs through recorded messages and support at virtual events. Their engagement survey at the end of 2020 reflected an increase in their inclusion sentiment, due at least in part to their Allyship Initiative.

Nancy achieved what she initially set out to do, but she acknowledged that there is still so much more work to be done. Only a subset of the company's employees has broad knowledge of allyship, so she will continue to build awareness of everyday actions to create momentum. While 2020 held many unexpected twists for the company's DEIB efforts, the resulting focus on fewer, more impactful initiatives allowed allyship to shine.

## What Each of Us Can Do

Allyship can be practiced in many different ways but it starts with educating yourself. Read about the histories of the different peoples in your country. Deepen your understanding of the issues that are important to marginalized communities. Get as close as possible to them so that you can truly understand the nuances involved, and develop empathy and compassion for the people who are affected.

As John Chambers, CEO of Cisco, said at his Cisco Impact keynote in 2019, "Get close to a problem and you will be compelled to try and solve it."[2] Bryan Stevenson, the renowned civil rights activist and founder of the Equal Justice Initiative, connects this even more strongly to DEIB: "We have to commit ourselves to getting proximate to the poor, to the excluded, to the marginalized. When you are proximate, details emerge, insights emerge, understandings emerge, that you will not achieve from a distance. There is power in proximity."[3] The closer we are to the issues, the more likely we are to be able to reflect on our own role in solving them.

This is one reason why I try to get every leader involved in DEIB initiatives by increasing their exposure to people who are not like them. I remember taking a sociology class in college that had an assignment for everyone to go somewhere outside of their normal day-to-day and experience a different culture than their norm.

I chose to attend an LGBT organization's annual picnic gathering for its members, one of whom was my brother, where I unexpectedly was asked out on a date by a lesbian who didn't realize I was there as an ally. I felt uncomfortable having to tell her that and had to reckon with the sense that I was intruding on their safe space as an outsider.

This was a great lesson in how it can feel to be an outsider in a different context, when your in-group status isn't something that can be visibly seen. And how careful you have to be as an ally to make sure you signal that you are there for support and not to co-opt their space for your own issues.

I suggest this exercise to everyone now. If you're white, attend some Black ERG events. If you're able-bodied, shadow a person with a mobility disability to understand their challenges throughout the workplace. Reverse-mentorship programs where you pair senior executives with people who are different from them so that the executives can learn more about marginalized communities can be extremely helpful to implement. These are all ways to get more proximate to different experiences and help increase your capability to be more inclusive of them in your day-to-day life.

Another way to demonstrate allyship is through amplification. This is when you use your power or platform to highlight underrepresented groups that may be overlooked by others.

During the Obama administration, women on his White House staff did this for each other to great success. When Obama first took office, two-thirds of his top aides were men, and women felt they were being ignored. So they started amplifying each others' voices by making sure that if a woman made a key point in a meeting, others in the meeting would repeat the point and give that woman credit for the idea. When Obama entered his second term, women were represented in equal proportion to men among his inner circle.[4] This is one way to amplify.

Another very practical thing I ask people to do is to review their social media networks. Who is in their LinkedIn connections? Whom do they follow on Twitter? What Instagram accounts do they click the like button on? Each of these platforms are an opportunity to amplify voices that wouldn't otherwise get as much visibility. The more people can ensure a diversity of voices in their social networks and work to highlight and share those voices, the more all of us can help those voices be heard and valued.

Conversely, if someone doesn't accept your invitation to connect or want to educate you on their experiences, don't take it personally and don't push the issue. Many marginalized people are just tired of all the work it takes to engage with others on DEIB, and we should respect that.

Lastly, action and intervention are necessary to being a good ally. It's not enough to stand in solidarity with a marginalized community. You have to be an upstander who takes action. You have to call out toxic workplaces that don't value the contributions of underrepresented groups and work to change them.

There were many statements by companies supporting Black Lives Matter after George Floyd's murder. That was great, but more importantly, many companies announced initiatives to invest in Black-owned businesses, set goals for more supplier diversity, and formed racial justice task forces to tackle racism internally. Netflix announced plans to move $100 million to financial institutions that serve the Black community.[5] Goldman Sachs has committed $10 billion to investing in Black women-led organizations.[6] Adidas has committed to the goal that 30 percent of all open positions will be filled by Black or Latinx talent.[7] As individuals, each of us can do something similar by buying from Black-owned businesses, donating to organizations supporting social justice, and speaking up when we see injustice happening. Together, we can all make a difference.

## PUTTING IT INTO ACTION

Using the template in Table 5.2, list the four allyship roles. List your various DEIB initiatives in the column heads.

For each initiative, who is the key influencer for each of these roles? What actions will you ask them to take as allies?

Table 5.2  **Ally Roles: Who Is Your Key Influencer, and What Do You Need from Them?**

| Ally Role | DEIB Initiative 1 | DEIB Initiative 2 | DEIB Initiative 3 |
|-----------|-------------------|-------------------|-------------------|
| Sponsor | | | |
| Amplifier | | | |
| Upstander | | | |
| Confidante | | | |

## KEY TAKEAWAYS

1. Position your ERGs as business resource groups with strategic plans, professional development, and rewards, not as unpaid volunteer opportunities.

2. Create a clear operating structure, expectations, and decision-making guidelines for ERGs to accomplish their objectives.

3. Define ally roles clearly so people can understand where to plug in.

4. Allyship starts with proximity. Get as close as you can to marginalized communities. Understand their history and their issues so you can advocate for them effectively.

5. Learn how to be an upstander and take action when you see the need.

# CHAPTER 6

# Navigating Risk

A t one company, I had to present a business case to a leadership team for diversity, and I was told I had to bring all the data. After I presented it, I was peppered with questions like, "How recent is that research?" "When was the data snapshot taken?" "Can you find case studies more relevant to our business?"

Like a good employee, I went back to my desk and gathered more data to answer all their questions. A month later I presented again to the leadership team. Then they asked more questions like, "Can you take a deeper dive into the applicant funnel data?" "What does our promotion data look like?" "How are we tracking succession planning?"

And the cycle repeated itself. After the third presentation over six months, I realized we were in a state of data analysis paralysis, unable to move forward out of fear of doing the wrong thing and using the lack of data as an excuse for inaction. It was incredibly frustrating. And I realized that I had fallen into one of the most common pitfalls to avoid in driving DEIB progress.

# DON'T CONFUSE INTENT WITH IMPACT

Unfortunately, DEIB is full of many failures like this. How else to explain the ongoing inequalities we see in our society? While many people truly believe in the need for more diversity, equity, inclusion, and belonging inside companies, their intent does not equal impact. We have to recognize when our actions, or lack thereof, are not producing the results we intend and course correct when necessary.

I've mentioned in previous chapters a few of the mistakes I've made. Generally speaking, though, there are some categories of mistakes that I've seen happen so many times that it's important to highlight them so you can identify when it's happening to you and work to mitigate the risk of such pitfalls so you can continue to move forward.

## Show Me the Data

*Data analysis paralysis* is an affliction that many business leaders experience. I am a big proponent of using data to inform decision-making. Every DEIB assessment should start with looking at your data on representation and shoring up your systems and processes as needed to help you get the data you need on your employee demographics and monitor them over time. Having good data will help you focus on the right things and drive better actions. But when the lack of data cripples you into inaction, it's time to start looking in the mirror at what might truly be holding you back and develop alternative ways to address the issue.

Over the years, I have done my fair share of gathering the data, doing the assessments, highlighting the latest research, and connecting the dots to the business in presentations galore to executives. But data can be manipulated, and research can have holes poked in it, and as a result, I have found myself in endless debates about the merit of this particular statistic versus that one. It's not very productive. I've discovered that to really move people to action, you can't just connect to their brains on a rational level. You have to also connect to their hearts at an emotional level.

After learning this lesson, the next time I presented a diversity strategy, I applied it to the discussion. I arrived to the meeting with my slides and data because they are the table stakes needed to prove your credibility with senior leaders. But that's not what I focused my messaging on. Instead, I talked at length about why it mattered from a personal perspective, and I shared a story about my brothers and how, when we don't champion diversity, it leaves people feeling like they are "less than," whether that's less competent, less valued, or less worthy. When I was done, it turned out I had moved a couple of people to tears. My first reaction was, "Oh, no! I didn't mean to do that!" but then my second reaction was, "Yes! Something I said deeply resonated, and I hope it was enough to get them to do something different."

It was. We finally stopped talking about the data and started talking about our action plan. Several members of the executive team signed on to sponsor employee resource groups, I got the budget I needed to implement more training, and they agreed to send staff to some upcoming recruiting conferences targeting underrepresented groups.

## Not Enough Time or Resources

Once you've moved your leaders into action though, it isn't all easy street. Now you have to be cautious of the pendulum swinging too far in the other direction, where leaders across the company are so focused on seeing results that they do not give their initiatives enough time or resources to work. A prime example of this is *recruiting conference sponsorships*.

One tech company I worked with had already been sponsoring the Anita Borg Institute's Grace Hopper Conference, the largest annual conference for women technologists globally, for four years running, spending at least $25,000 per year. But they had managed to get zero hires from the sponsorship during all that time. Looking into this more deeply, I discovered that our presence at the conference each year consisted of a couple of recruiters holding down a small booth, while a few women employees attended separately and with no cross-coordination efforts.

We also never had major speaking roles at the conference, which are critical for signaling to attendees that we had women technologists in senior technical roles that they could aspire to at our company as well. While I was under budget pressure to discontinue the sponsorship, it was very apparent that we hadn't put in the right level of resources to ensure that this partnership would give us a return on our investment.

To encourage applications, I partnered with our women in technology ERG to get the word out that we would fund the travel for anyone who was accepted as a speaker at the next conference. We also put one of our executives on the speaker selection committee to support the visibility of our speaker applicants. I asked several senior technical executives to send as many of our female technologists to the conference as they could afford and to market the opportunity aggressively within their organizations.

I facilitated a stronger partnership between our women in tech ERG and our recruiting team to make sure we leveraged those who were attending the conference to help staff our recruiting booth, which we increased to three times the previous size. It was imperative that we develop a process to interview for roles on-site, send hiring managers to the conference for this purpose, and follow up quickly afterward with job offers. I canvased three organizations to fund an increase of our sponsorship level to three times our previous level, which also gave us the opportunity to have our CEO as one of the keynote speakers at the conference.

These combined efforts led us to make 14 offers to women technologists attending the conference, which resulted in seven hires into internship or entry-level positions—a small start but a significant leap forward from zero.

In a world where short-term thinking is rewarded more often than long-term gain, it can be difficult to stay the course on DEIB initiatives when they don't seem to be yielding any significant results. But it's important to understand that if your company hasn't embarked on a DEIB strategy before and, therefore, hasn't built up any credibility in supporting marginalized communities beyond the occasional donation or sponsorship, you cannot expect people to immediately trust that you truly care about correcting systemic inequality.

While marginalized communities will be grateful that you've turned your attention to them, you still need to prove to them that you are in it for the long haul because they have been burned in the past by too many false promises of support. Commit to a few targeted organizations for at least three years, and build a deep relationship with those organizations such that you are true partners collaborating on how to increase opportunities for those who have been historically shut out. And dedicate the right resources to these partnerships to really make them work. Otherwise, you are setting yourself up for failure.

## DEIB as Side Hustle

This leads us to another common mistake that many companies make: treating DEIB as a side hustle as opposed to being a core part of their business. According to Josh Bersin's 2021 study on effective DEI practices within companies, "Elevating Equity and Diversity: The Challenge of the Decade," the organizations that are highest performing are the ones that run DEI as a business function and work to ensure that it is sustainable over time.[1]

These are the firms that build DEI into all processes as an outcome and share accountability for it at all levels. As a result, they are 4.6 times more likely to satisfy and retain customers and almost twice as likely to excel financially than companies that don't. When DEIB is a side hustle, you might as well call it "window dressing," where you put out words of commitment and a façade of caring about DEIB when in reality, you're not willing to make the changes, dedicate the resources, or prioritize the actions necessary to build a real workplace culture of inclusion.

You may be able to attract diversity into your firm because of the welcoming messages you put out on social media and the diverse faces you put on your website, but you won't be able to keep that diversity once the new hires realize they aren't in an inclusive environment with equitable opportunities after all. So you get the zero progress result highlighted earlier in the Diversity Equation.

I have unfortunately been in these situations, despite my best efforts to identify a deeper commitment to DEIB before saying yes to a contract or role. It's difficult to discern because when you ask how committed leaders are to DEIB action, everyone will nod their heads and agree that diversity and inclusion are important and that we should do something to improve both. But the reality is, who's not going to say that?

You have to go deeper to understand whether the commitment is real. A flawed commitment will show up in several ways. If you treat DEIB more as risk management and compliance programs rather than a business imperative, that is a red flag.

In my career, I have worked with a few senior executives whose highest priority was minimizing risk for their firms. They initially saw DEIB work as aligned with risk management in that if you create a truly inclusive environment, you will decrease the potential for discrimination lawsuits. And as long as my work as the DEI leader stayed in what they deemed "safe" areas that didn't touch on controversial topics or raise the possibility of someone recognizing that they were not treated equitably, then we got along great. But inevitably, there was tension every time I pushed them to consider an action that was outside of their comfort zone of risk, such as celebrating transgender expression at work. We were all trying to do what we thought was best for the company, yet sometimes it's necessary to take on some risk in order to achieve the DEIB outcomes that the company is prioritizing.

This has meant that I have clashed with executives over efforts to roll out antiracism training, the need to solicit feedback from employees on whether they felt a company's environment was inclusive, and how to increase transparency and accountability around our data and goals, among many other examples. My ability to make progress was limited by low levels of risk tolerance.

The issue with this approach is that employees can see when progress isn't happening and will either call you out on it or leave. More often than not, if you see an attrition issue among underrepresented groups, it means you are not living up to your stated commitment, and you should probably have an open dialogue with your company's leaders to be honest about where you stand.

## No Follow-Through

Another sign of a flawed commitment is a *lack of follow-through*, which is easy to spot. It usually shows up like this: I've gotten agreement on an action plan, and I go back to the leadership team in three months to monitor progress, but nothing's been done. So I ask why, and I get excuses like, "I just need to wrap up the quarter, and then I can focus on it" or, "My biggest issue right now is getting product out the door so let's talk once that's done."

Probably the most egregious version of this that I've experienced so far in my career was when I asked to present the DEI strategy at the CEO's staff meeting. My leader agreed and said, "Let's put you on the next agenda." But then something came up, and I had to get rescheduled to the meeting after next. And then something else happened, and I couldn't present for another two months. This kept happening until fully six months had gone by and I still hadn't met with the CEO and his staff. That's when I knew there was no way I could be successful delivering strong DEIB results at that company.

*Stalling* is probably the most often employed tactic when a business leader is not ready to engage on DEIB yet. Another DEI colleague of mine detailed how, after being asked by her business leader for a DEI action plan, she was then asked for just the must-haves, before being asked for just the 30- and 60-day actions.

At that point, she realized the pattern and decided to move on and work on things that were within her control. These stalling behaviors will often happen when leaders aren't ready to emotionally engage with the work or are too afraid of what the work will entail. If you find yourself in one of these patterns, make sure you confront what is going on and get to the root of what the organization's leaders are truly willing to do. If they cannot move past their hesitancy, then you have to make a decision to continue working on what you can really influence or put your efforts elsewhere.

## Ready, Fire, Aim!

On the other hand, another mistake I see companies make is nearly the polar opposite, when they actually jump into action without thinking it through or connecting it to a broader DEIB strategy. Which in and of itself, isn't a terrible thing as some action in support of DEIB is often better than no action, as long as it isn't harmful to the communities we're trying to support.

But when it is part of a set of actions that focuses only on helping people feel better because they are doing something, rather than actions that are actually meant to make a real difference to DEIB, then it becomes a "check-the-box" activity that feels performative rather than authentic in its intent to drive inclusive change.

After the murder of George Floyd in 2020, many business leaders felt a need to do something to address the racism against Black people that the video highlighted. All the social media statements, commitments to stop racism, and donations to organizations supporting anti-racist efforts were great, but what were companies doing to dismantle the systemic racism that existed within their own organizations? What meaningful actions were they taking internally to support their Black employees?

Every DEIB training consultant I knew was inundated with calls, and it became impossible to book a training session without at least three months' lead time. Yet, it seemed like very few companies were actually addressing what comes after the training. Delivering bias training to employees felt like it was just checking a box to show employees that they were doing something.

As mentioned in Chapter 4, companies doing the real work know that training is only one component of a comprehensive DEIB strategy that needs to happen to make change stick. DEIB training needs to be ongoing because our understanding of what it takes to be effective is constantly evolving and we need to refresh our knowledge and skill sets periodically to stay up-to-date. And it needs to be paired with the programs, accountability, infrastructure, and technology to support addressing the DEIB four *P*s Inclusion Ecosystem as a whole.

Lastly, it will be futile to try to make progress in DEIB without doing the inner work required to mitigate our own biases in parallel. We have to be self-aware enough to realize when our biases might be affecting our work so that we can put in place the mechanisms to disrupt it. We have to be humble enough to realize that we don't know all the answers and work to educate ourselves on DEIB issues through reading, conversation, and examination. We have to be bold enough to change our behaviors when they don't serve the greater goals of DEIB and let go of old habits even when it's uncomfortable, like replacing "you guys" with "y'all," or asking people if they'd like to disclose the pronouns they use before starting a meeting (pro tip: don't make it mandatory or you might accidentally out someone before they're ready). If we don't take the time or energy to unpack the stereotypes we've internalized within ourselves, it will be very difficult to ask others to unpack theirs.

## Putting It into Action

Take the self-assessment for DEI excellence in Table 6.1. If you score 35+, you're doing well. If you score 25 to 34, then you have a bit of work to do. For scores below 25, you need to make some significant changes in order to drive progress.

### Table 6.1 Organizational Self-Assessment

| DEI Excellence Factor | Score (1 to 5 from Strongly Disagree to Strongly Agree) |
| --- | --- |
| DEIB is core to our business. | |
| Our senior leaders are deeply committed to DEIB. | |
| We have well-defined DEIB goals and actions. | |
| We have communicated our DEIB goals and actions to our key stakeholders. | |
| We review progress on our DEIB goals and actions on a regular basis. | |
| We recognize and reward people who contribute significantly to DEIB as a priority. | |
| We have a dedicated team and budget for DEIB. | |

| We have integrated a DEIB lens into all of our talent processes (for example, hiring, development, talent review, and succession planning). | |
|---|---|
| Our benefits and policies are very inclusive. | |
| We regularly gather key stakeholder input on our DEIB efforts. | |

# LEGAL ISN'T THE LAST WORD

Another risk area for DEIB work that has to be navigated effectively is legal liability. In doing DEIB work, legal can be both your biggest ally and your biggest roadblock. For leaders who are risk averse or not motivated to tackle DEIB, having legal requirements to do so may be the only way to motivate action. For leaders who are trying to be progressive and innovative in how they solve their DEIB issues, legal risk must be balanced with the need to do the unconventional.

I have seen many business leaders become too paralyzed to act when legal advises against something. Employment counsel is paid to help businesses avoid the risk of litigation around potential discrimination issues, and they are motivated to look for reasons not to share demographic data that could be used against the company in discrimination claims, or not to focus a program on an underrepresented group if it could be seen as reverse discrimination.

These are good things to be aware of as you make decisions on how to drive DEIB progress. However, you have to weigh these risks against the potential for progress. Companies have been doing what's "safe" for the last 50 years, and we've made little progress. It's time for companies to make bolder moves and to stand up for their values and commitments to DEIB in a way that doesn't reinforce the status quo. Companies are starting to recognize this and moving forward accordingly.

Prior to 2014, Google, along with several other prominent tech companies, had categorically declined to share their demographic numbers on the grounds that it would do them competitive harm. Yet when Google finally decided in that year to share its demographic numbers in an effort to be more open and accountable to improving the company's diversity numbers,[2] this was seen as a bold move that launched a trend around transparency that many other tech companies have since followed. This disclosure has also spurred companies in other industries to share their diversity data too.

You will also have to decide where you fall on the risk spectrum. Are you willing to risk potential lawsuits to be more transparent around your diversity data and hopefully drive more progress? Do you want to arm your business leaders with enough data and insights to focus on informed actions that can be measured and tracked? Or do you want them to take actions that are more like a shot in the dark and may or may not get the results you are hoping for?

The latter is what many companies do today when they don't give business leaders the information they need to understand where underrepresented groups might be falling out of the hiring process or why they might be leaving the company at a higher rate than others. Yes, sharing more information with more people means greater risk of that information being used in unintended ways that could harm the company, but if you believe you are making your best efforts to address DEIB issues and that the benefits of doing so outweighs the risks, then it's important to move your DEIB efforts forward in a way that is still legally defensible by your company.

I have had the good fortune to work with some of the most progressive employment lawyers in the country. When you have a great legal partner who supports DEIB, they can help you address risk concerns effectively and accelerate progress.

We all have choices to make. We can look at the example of State Street Global Advisors (SSGA), which created their Fearless Girl campaign around a statue of a girl installed in front of the New York Stock Exchange that started a global conversation about the need for more women in leadership and has prompted 862 companies so far to add women to their boards of directors.[3] That same year, State Street settled a gender pay discrimination lawsuit for $5 million alleging that they were paying female and Black executives less than their white male colleagues.[4]

Although the lawsuit started long before State Street launched its Fearless Girl campaign, to some people, this highlighted the legal risk of touting a company's DEIB commitment very publicly. Once you're known for having some success in the DEIB space, you become a target for lawsuits from those whose experiences with your company are felt to be different than the perception.

You could view this as a cautionary tale to not talk about your DEIB efforts, let alone mount a public campaign that would invite not only criticism and scrutiny but also potentially cost a large sum of money and cause irreparable damage to your company's reputation. Or you could see this as owning your mistakes and then doing what's right and understanding that the cost of not having women in leadership roles at companies will far outstrip what you might pay in legal fees and is, therefore, worth it.

## Is It Reverse Discrimination?

The other way I often see legal risks arise in DEIB efforts is around programs that try to specifically target an underrepresented group, such as a leadership program for women or mentoring programs focused on Black and Brown communities. I have received legal advice saying that these programs should be open to everyone, that we can't have something only for an underrepresented group.

What this ignores is the fact that most existing leadership development programs are already implicitly targeting those in a majority group who have defined what leadership potential looks like. The scales are already tipped in favor of the white, male, and able-bodied majority within corporate America (and even more so if you're tall![5]). Programs targeting underrepresented groups are really seeking only to balance those scales.

That we would be more afraid of charges of reverse discrimination by those in power than we are of charges of discrimination by those not in power says a lot about which status quo we are more comfortable maintaining. We need to be brave enough to stand up for those with less privilege than ourselves and educate people on why targeted programs are necessary.

Having said that, it's also important to ensure that you set up and message these programs in a way that helps people understand we are striving for equal opportunity to participate. You could set up a general leadership program and have something supplemental for underrepresented groups. Or make sure upstander training is available to everyone, not just those in a majority group. Conduct pay equity audits for different dimensions of diversity and ensure that adjustments are made for anyone, whether in an underrepresented group or in a majority group, who falls outside of the expected pay range. There are multiple ways to demonstrate that you truly are driving for equity and leveling the playing field for all.

## Law Abiding or Not?

Another area that requires some legal navigation is affirmative action, which we first defined in Chapter 1. For many companies, their efforts around DEIB start from a compliance perspective. In the United States, any company that is a federal contractor with more than 50 employees is subject to the Office of Federal Contract Compliance Programs (OFCCP) rules and regulations.

Unfortunately, many of these rules and regulations won't actually support your DEIB efforts. While DEIB and affirmative action have the same end goals of achieving equal employment opportunity for everyone, how they get there can be vastly different. Affirmative action rules are primarily location based, and in today's world of remote working and business lines that are run across multiple locations but roll up into the same hierarchy, the rules can actually confuse things more than they can help.

While I consider affirmative action analyses to be good inputs to locally based DEIB plans, they aren't particularly helpful in holding business leaders accountable to closing representation gaps when they can't be applied to a specific business unit or function. And compliance with these rules can often mean more time is spent in documenting performative efforts rather than taking the actions needed to reach affirmative action goals.

It can be difficult to balance the need for compliance with how you actually run your business. I will often have multiple different diversity action plans to track in a single location because there are several lines of business responsible for that location. This usually means that a location council of business leaders must coordinate across the location to ensure that they are coordinated and not driving redundant efforts.

Sometimes, companies may find themselves in situations in which local laws conflict with their values. Global companies may operate in countries that outlaw LGBTQ+ orientations or don't support gender equality. These are situations in which companies must decide whether their values are more important than complying with unjust laws.

Can a company be a safe harbor for their LGBTQ+ employees when their country doesn't sanction their existence, without breaking local laws? Better yet, can a company use its economic clout to help change unjust laws?

We've seen examples of that happen in the United States. Salesforce canceled all programs requiring customers or employees to travel to Indiana in 2015 in the wake of the passing of the Religious Freedom Restoration Act that allowed businesses to discriminate based on religious beliefs against people who were LGBTQ+.[6] As a result of pressure like that among others, Indiana amended the bill to protect the LGBTQ+ community from discrimination under that law. These are tough issues on which business leaders will have to decide how far they are willing to go to support DEIB.

## PUTTING IT INTO ACTION

Using the template in Table 6.2, outline potential risks you might hear from legal on the action plan you outlined in Table 3.3 in Chapter 3.

- What potential risks do you anticipate?

- Are your leaders aligned?

- What is your level of risk tolerance?

- How will you mitigate these risks?

Table 6.2 **Risk Mitigation Planning**

| DEIB Actions | Potential Risks | Risk Level (High/ Medium/Low) | Mitigation Action |
|---|---|---|---|
|  |  |  |  |
|  |  |  |  |
|  |  |  |  |

# BRACE FOR BACKLASH

Whatever you decide as to whether and how your business will take a stand in support of DEIB, it's important to remember that there will be reactions both positive and negative to whatever you do. Progressives will say you're not doing enough, and conservatives will say you're doing far too much. This is not work for the faint of heart. You have to prepare yourself for the inevitable backlash you will experience to whatever you put out there. That backlash can take many different forms, either from your internal employees or from the external public.

## Center Inclusion Internally

Earlier I mentioned the legal risk of being accused of reverse discrimination, probably the most pervasive form of potential backlash you will encounter. This can range from the subtle, "I am white and I don't feel included," to the more inflammatory, "You promoted that female colleague over me when I was more qualified!" While every situation is unique and requires a thorough investigation into what the person in the majority party is perceiving and the facts pertaining to their particular allegations, there are ways to address this more proactively so that reverse discrimination doesn't rear its ugly head.

One way is to ensure that your ERGs are inclusive to all. While ERGs are formed to create safe spaces for people from underrepresented groups to connect and support each other, they can often be seen as exclusionary because they are focused around particular groups. That's why it's important to welcome people who do not necessarily share an affinity with that particular ERG into the group as part of maintaining our integrity with our value of inclusion as well as helping to educate potential allies on issues important to our underrepresented communities. And part of that education should include how the existence of

ERGs helps us to celebrate our differences in a way that unites us all rather than dividing us.

Another tactic is to engage directly with the person who is raising the issue. Many people in majority groups can be so used to being centered in every story that, when they are suddenly not centered in the diversity conversation, it can be really disconcerting for them. They may react with discomfort or guilt, feeling blamed for all the issues that underrepresented groups are experiencing. They may ask questions like, "Why isn't there an ERG for men?" or make comments like, "I think there should be a town hall about white culture since there was one about Black History Month."

It is crucial not to dismiss their feedback. Instead, engage them in a conversation so that they can better understand your response. You could say, "There is not an ERG for men because that is already the default at our company which has a majority male demographic. But they are welcome to start one as long as it fits in with the company's ERG guidelines supporting underrepresented groups."

You could add that there won't be a town hall about white culture because the majority of history classes and textbooks taught in the United States over the past century have already been focused on white culture. But if they feel there is a gap that they need to fill for others at the company, they are welcome to organize it in alignment with our core DEIB principle of highlighting marginalized voices and stories. I usually don't get a lot of follow-up on such requests after I have these conversations.

You also know from Chapter 5 that I believe broad education about what it means to be an ally can be really helpful. Highlighting the injustices that marginalized groups have experienced is not about blame. It is about increasing our collective understanding so that it can lead to more positive actions in the future that will right the wrongs of those injustices.

If you feel badly about those injustices, let's reframe that emotion as having empathy for a different lived experience than your own, which is a good thing to experience. And hopefully it can then motivate you to become an ally and actively hold yourself and others accountable to supporting marginalized communities. So don't be motivated by guilt. Be motivated by the shared responsibility we all have to contribute to an inclusive and equitable society.

On the other side of the spectrum are people who are trying to be well-meaning allies, but instead they actually harm your DEIB efforts. This usually happens because they are so concerned about fairness and equality and not from any kind of ill intent.

I was working with a diversity task force that wanted to implement a mentoring program specifically targeting underrepresented racial and/or ethnic minorities within its organization. But the executive in charge was worried about how it would be perceived by those who weren't being targeted by the program. "Isn't targeting a particular group over another inherently unfair?" he asked. "How does perpetuating inequality for the majority group advance an inclusion agenda?"

He genuinely wanted to resolve what had become a paradox in his mind. I had to explain to him that by not instituting such a program, we were already perpetuating inequality for the minority groups inside his organization that already clearly favored white males in its leadership ranks. The surprise on his face told me that my assertion was something he hadn't considered before. So I asked him to reframe the mentoring program not as favoring one group over another but, rather, as correcting for an existing bias that favored the status quo.

I also pointed out that the mentoring program was inclusive of everyone—anyone within the organization could apply to be in it. I said that we were just calling out that we wanted a significant number of people from underrepresented racial and/or ethnic minorities to participate, and we asked all managers to encourage their top talent, especially their underrepresented top talent, to apply. This resulted in almost all of the organization's racial and/or ethnic minority top talent participating in the mentoring program.

I try not to see internal resistance to DEIB efforts as blockers because in the end, addressing people's concerns almost always results in more buy-in and more effective efforts.

## Nothing About Us Without Us

In corporations that are used to a top-down, command-and-control way of doing things, DEIB efforts will often receive backlash, not from their employees, but from their company leaders instead. It's really difficult to make any progress in this type of environment unless your leaders understand that they cannot apply a top-down approach to DEIB. As mentioned in Chapter 2, being inclusive of other viewpoints means involving people from your marginalized communities in the process of making decisions that affect those communities.

I worked with one leadership team that developed a DEIB strategy supporting the Black community but fully ignored feedback on the strategy from their Black employees. The leaders truly believed they knew what kinds of initiatives were best for the company to engage in because that's how they had risen to become leaders at the company.

What they did not understand was how, because their team members were all white, making decisions on strategies that affected the Black community without their input called to mind the US racial history of slavery when white slave owners made all the decisions about their Black slaves. It is an entirely different context today, but the dynamic felt too similar.

Needless to say, their decisions did not go over well with the community they were actually trying to support. When this happens, it's best to be honest with your leaders about the reasons behind the reaction. And ensure that they change their decision-making process when it comes to DEIB issues or risk undermining their ability to achieve their DEIB commitments.

## Handling External Incidents

Despite your best DEIB efforts, every organization is only one incident away from a PR debacle that tests its values and resolve in supporting DEIB. When Susan Fowler wrote a 2,900-word essay about the sexism she experienced while working at Uber and published it to her blog in February 2017, I doubt anyone thought it would gain so much steam that it would eventually result in Travis Kalanick, the CEO of Uber at the time, being forced out of the company he both founded and grew into a transportation behemoth.[7]

Uber's initial response to Susan Fowler's post was to promise an independent investigation led by Attorney General Eric Holder and one of their board members, Arianna Huffington, cofounder of the *Huffington Post*. The investigation resulted in sweeping changes at the company, including the aforementioned leadership change, as well as the appointment of a new chief diversity officer, new HR systems and processes for handling complaints, and stronger board oversight of the firm's diversity and inclusion efforts.[8]

This was a powerful change to how Uber had previously handled sexist incidents inside the firm. Acknowledging the concerns raised and taking strong actions to address them started Uber down the path of repairing the negative impacts to their business. Events like these are next to impossible to predict, but we all know they can happen to any company. And with the increasing influence of social media and movements like #MeToo and #BlackLivesMatter, it is so much easier for stories like these to come out and go viral.

My best advice is to try to be proactive in imagining a worst-case scenario along these lines and drafting a response plan so your teams aren't caught off guard when something does happen. Know who your key partners will be in addressing incidents like these, and prep them with scenario simulations to develop a playbook to work from.

And if this does happen to your company, you can use it to learn from your mistakes. Many people will forgive one incident, but if you are a repeat offender, your business is likely to suffer as a result. In 2002, Abercrombie & Fitch (A&F) sold T-shirts that said, "Wong Brothers Laundry Service—Two Wongs Can Make It White," among other Asian stereotype-reinforcing caricatures and sayings. This prompted a media firestorm that resulted in A&F pulling those shirts from stores.[9]

But in 2005, they sold women's T-shirts that had "With these, who needs brains?" printed on them, prompting a protest organized by a teen girl group in Pennsylvania. The group's protest gained enough media attention that A&F pulled those shirts from their shelves as well.[10] This was in addition to being sued for racial discrimination in hiring and being called out for not carrying plus sizes in their stores.

Their CEO at the time appeared to not take these issues very seriously. Sales at the retailer had already been falling since the end of the 2000s. In 2017 the company installed a new CEO and added more gender diversity to its leadership team, and the company was poised for a comeback prior to the pandemic.[11] Was this a coincidence or a result of a stronger focus on inclusivity? You get to decide.

### PUTTING IT INTO ACTION

Put together a crisis response plan, using the guide in Table 6.3.

### Table 6.3 Crisis Response Plan

| Stakeholders | Whom do I need to pull in? |
|---|---|
| | • Corporate communications |
| | • Diversity task force or council |
| | • ERG if relevant |
| | • Human resources and/or employee relations |
| | • Legal |
| | • Customer experience if relevant |
| | • Government affairs |

| Decision makers | Who needs to approve our response?<br>• Board members<br>• CEO<br>• Other executives |
|---|---|
| Timing | What do we have to do now versus later?<br>• Immediate<br>• Short term<br>• Long term |
| Process | What is our process to get to a recommended response?<br>• Rapid response team<br>• CEO staff meeting<br>• External consultants |
| Communication plan | What will we communicate, to whom, how, and when?<br>• Audiences<br>• Communication objectives<br>• Key messages<br>• Channels—internal or external<br>• Timing<br>• Owners and/or authors |
| Actions | What actions will make up the substance of our response?<br>• What can you accelerate?<br>• What needs to be deprioritized?<br>• What can you expand? |
| Potential impact | How will we know we achieved our response goals?<br>• Measures of success<br>• Who is affected |
| Follow-up | How will we demonstrate accountability for our response?<br>• Communications<br>• Progress<br>• Anything else |

## KEY TAKEAWAYS

1. Navigating and balancing risk effectively with your ability to drive impact will make or break your progress in DEIB.

2. Avoid doing what feels good instead of what will make substantive impact in DEIB. Take action against the pitfalls of data analysis paralysis, lack of time and resources for DEIB, treating DEIB as a side hustle, or lack of follow-through.

3. Make friends with your legal partners. Ensure that they have the same goals as you in driving DEIB.

4. Backlash will happen so be prepared for it, both internally and externally.

5. Responding to external crisis events with empathy, integrity, and action is important to amplify your DEIB efforts. How you respond can be a catalyst for progress or set you back a few years.

## CHAPTER 7

# Measuring Success

In every interview I've had for a DEIB role, the question has come up about what results I was able to produce at the company I was at. How much progress did you drive? How did you measure success? What results did your initiatives achieve? And after I share some impressive numbers, the next question is always, *how* did you do that? My reply has been that I always start with envisioning the answers to the questions about results *before* I launch any new DEIB initiative. While defining these results and how to measure them up front can add to the design and development time for initiatives, I believe it's the best way to ensure that all stakeholders are aligned with and motivated to drive the outcomes I'm striving for.

Once you've put together your goals, strategies, and programs, the final step is defining what success looks like. There are lots of different metrics you can use to help you understand your progress. I'll touch on some of the more common ones here. What you use is dependent both on the maturity of your systems and processes for collecting data and what your DEIB initiatives are. It's also just as important to include both quantitative and qualitative measures. Quantitative data will give you the hard metrics you need to understand whether you are achieving the outcomes you are striving for in your organization, and qualitative data will give you the directional insight that can explain what is going on either behind the numbers or in the absence of being able to collect hard data.

## WHAT GETS MEASURED GETS DONE

Representation is probably the most basic quantitative metric of success in DEIB and foundational to your ability to measure progress across the four *P*s of people, place, product, and planet. There are two levels of representation important to pay attention to. First, do you have diversity in the demographics represented at your company? At a minimum, you should be looking at your company's makeup of gender, age, and race and/or ethnicity. For companies in the United States, you also have the option to collect and review military status and disability status. Beyond that, you can ask for voluntary identification of gender identity, sexual orientation, caregiver status, nationality, or whatever other dimension of diversity you feel it is necessary to focus your initiatives on.

Secondly, are your demographics at parity with your available talent pools? To achieve equity, closing the gap between your company's internal demographics and external available talent pools is a necessary step. It can be tricky to determine what your available talent pools are for specific roles because government-tracked data is often not as granular as what we would define potential candidates for a job to be, but when it comes to diversity data, it is never going to be 100 percent perfect.

Self-identification data gathering should be completely voluntary. That means you can't require people to disclose how they identify. You can only encourage it by sharing how important it is to self-identify and how the data will be kept confidential and used only to make progress on your DEIB efforts. People will still decline to identify, not understand the terminology, skip the questions altogether, or even intentionally misidentify because they don't trust how the data will be used.

But we have to move forward with what we're able to gather and not let the lack of data undermine the sustainability of DEIB efforts. So I look at representation by different locations, job levels, business units, and functions and any other cut that is important to how talent moves through the organization. This gives me a good idea of what our current state is and where we need to go from there.

The last thing I'll mention about representation is the importance of not "othering" people. When you list different options for self-identification, you need to make sure you are not listing "other" at the bottom of the list of choices you offer. "Other" can be interpreted as not belonging. So you'll want to either provide a free form field where people can type in how they identify, or replace "other" with something like "not listed" or "I use a different category."

Representation is also a metric you need to examine at every stage of the employee life cycle. In hiring, it's important to look at how diversity moves through your entire hiring funnel, from applicants to recruiter screen to on-site interviews to offer acceptance. If you see narrowing of your demographic pipeline at each stage, that is a red flag that there is bias in the system that needs to be addressed. If you see similar proportional demographics throughout each stage of hiring, then you've got some good indication of an inclusive hiring process.

When you compare this analysis with your current representation, it's usually easy to see how hiring practices lead to any issues you see with representation. In one company, the entire leadership team for the engineering function was from a single demographic, all South Asian men, which was not representative of the rest of the organization. Clearly, there was a bias for people with this particular background that was manifesting itself in our hiring criteria and needed to be addressed.

A senior diversity leader with a career spanning different global companies across different industries shared with me how she implemented DEIB metrics from scratch in some organizations and refreshed them in others. Let's call her Janelle. In all cases, Janelle's goal was to be able to tell if they were making progress in their DEIB efforts.

The thing to remember about metrics is that they are not the end-all or be-all of the DEIB goals you are driving. At best, they are indicators of your progress along a few fronts, which hopefully will give you an idea of how you're doing in general. At worst, they become the only conversation, and they distort the effort around DEIB.

Some metrics she recommended tracking related to representation of women (globally) and race and/or ethnicity (United States):

- Current representation and historical trend

- Representation of hires (including candidate slate)

- Representation of departures (voluntary and involuntary)

The most frequent views she has used for gender and race and/or ethnicity include breakouts by level, by location, and by next-level managers. She recommended looking at this alongside workforce planning, company location strategy, and business strategy.

Why look at all of this together? If a specific organization is in a steady state with low growth, it's not the place where you want to implement a new talent acquisition diversity program. It can sometimes be helpful to look at locations or regions that are high growth and target the organizations that make up the bulk of the site. This is particularly powerful if you have a regional or site-specific team that is motivated and supportive of DEIB.

## How to Measure Belonging

*Attrition* is another key performance indicator for DEIB efforts. If you see disproportionate numbers of underrepresented groups leaving the organization, that could be signaling an inclusion and belonging issue that bears further research and analysis. Isolating whether the attrition is being driven by a specific organization or manager can be particularly insightful. I also pay attention to exit interview themes and surveys quite closely.

Often, I will conduct a series of exit interviews with people from underrepresented groups when I see a spiking trend in order to better understand what is going on and how I might address it. If you have built credibility and trust, and people feel psychologically safe to express their true experiences and feelings with you, these interviews can be truly rich sources of information.

When I heard that women were leaving our sales organization at a disproportionately high rate in a relatively condensed period of time, I reached out to each one who had left in the previous three months and had an in-depth conversation with them on why they left. Their exit surveys all said they left for career development reasons. But in their interviews, they told me they felt that their careers were going nowhere because of the bias against women in the function, where they were often asked to do the "office housework" of taking notes during meetings or cleaning up after them, or they were passed over for promotions multiple times by men who didn't produce as much, yet were more chummy with their supervisors. It was eye-opening for the functional leaders to hear this, and we decided to implement some targeted interventions to ensure that men and women were treated and evaluated more fairly and equitably.

Using *employee engagement* or *diversity climate surveys* is also extremely helpful in measuring inclusion, equity, and belonging. When you ask people DEIB-focused survey questions, you invite them to reflect on their specific experiences and express them in a channel that feels safe. You should also analyze your survey data by the different demographics in your current state to detect differences in experiences between groups.

That's where real insight comes in. Working with my analytics partners, I try to create a *heat map* of leaders across the organization who score high and low on perceptions of inclusion and belonging by their teams. This tells me whom I can tap as a role model for others and better understand their best practices so I can replicate them across the organization. I can also see what leaders I need to focus on to stage interventional actions and help them adopt some of those best practices.

These types of measures should be factored into your managers' performance evaluations as well. If managers aren't demonstrating inclusive leadership skills, they likely aren't being as effective as they could be in other aspects of their role. Being a former survey researcher, though, I implore you to make sure you're using effective survey questions that truly get at what you're trying to measure. Don't just put together a list of questions that come top of mind for you.

I say this because I have learned the hard way that your outputs are only as good as your inputs, meaning that if you ask bad questions, you will get bad data. Many survey companies share the kinds of questions they use to better understand inclusion, equity, and belonging, and I encourage you to leverage these kinds of resources to help you construct a valid survey instrument. Culture Amp is one such company that has released an entire toolkit that can help you understand how people from all groups feel about your company's workplace.[1]

## Lagging or Leading Indicators

The unfortunate thing about most of these metrics is that they are *lagging indicators* rather than *leading indicators*. Meaning they tell you about problems after the fact rather than giving you enough information to fix a problem before it happens. That is why you should invest in a *people analytics function* at your organization if you haven't already.

I cannot overstate the value of having a good people analytics partner for DEIB work. When I had the opportunity to work with some highly competent data scientists, we created a predictive model to help us identify the organizational factors that contribute to disengagement that could ultimately lead to higher attrition among our underrepresented groups.

When we aggregated attrition, representation, and employee engagement data and correlated it with over 40 organizational factors, we determined that people who had more than two manager changes over the course of a year were at high risk for disengagement and attrition. So we could actually develop a plan to minimize the impact of organizational shifts like this. And we worked directly with leaders in organizations that were going through restructuring to effectively manage those changes and prevent disengagement.

Another good gauge of how your company is doing on inclusion and belonging is how well your employee resource groups are doing. You can look at their levels of membership, number of activities, attendance at events, types of activities they engage in, and what kind of impact they are having on the business from a hiring, advancement, and customer engagement perspective.

Probably the most difficult area for ERGs to measure is impact because it's a more nascent expectation for ERGs and so many of them are just learning how to lead in this respect. Also, internal systems are rarely set up to support measuring ERG impact from the beginning. You will have to spend time and effort integrating things like adding ERGs as a source of referrals to applicant-tracking systems or marking hiring events as ERG supported in other internal tracking documents.

We worked with our ERGs in one company to develop educational seminars geared specifically toward an underserved demographic, like women or LGBTQ+. The goal was to implement these educational seminars across our sales force, training them to deliver the seminars countrywide and bringing in new clients as a result. But in order to track how many clients we acquired from these seminars, we had to build new fields in our customer acquisition–tracking system and train our salespeople to make sure they tracked things appropriately. This was critical to our ability to show that the ERGs were contributing directly to business revenue outcomes.

## Regular Feedback Loops

I also encourage regular focus groups or interviews across your company to understand how your company messages are being received. Having leaders facilitate roundtables with members of underrepresented groups is a great way to create proximity to the issues and have them demonstrate their commitment to DEIB. Just the act of asking people what they think about various DEIB issues goes a long way toward building trust and credibility in this space.

It always floors me when people tell me how grateful they are that we are even asking them for their perspectives about DEIB, especially in companies that haven't done it before. This reinforces for me the belief that people at a bare minimum want to be seen and heard. Validating their perspectives in this way gives them confidence that you truly care. Just remember that confidence is not enough. You have to demonstrate courage, accountability, respect, and empowerment (CARE) and address their concerns with actions in some way to do more than just check the box.

It's also important to monitor your feedback channels from employees for sentiment on how you're doing and what else needs to be addressed. For example, if you have a practice of weekly all-hands meetings, then monitoring and tracking any questions related to DEIB that come up in that channel will tell you what is on employees' minds and how well any previous DEIB communications have landed.

Similarly, if you have internal group chat mechanisms that are open to anyone from the company to comment on, then it's useful to read what's being talked about in those groups to understand whether your initiative landed as intended or caused a stir of some kind. Whenever an external event such as a racially motivated hate crime garners significant media coverage and affects a proportion of your employees, tracking the kinds of requests and feedback that come to the DEIB team will also help you gauge the effectiveness of your response.

Lastly, embarking on a regular listening tour across the organization and getting leadership feedback on what they're hearing from employees and how different programs have rolled out are extremely helpful to rounding out whatever data picture you are able to see.

## Other Considerations

Beyond what I've outlined so far, there are a whole host of potential metrics you could monitor for success. What you focus on should be directly related to what your DEIB strategy and initiatives are and built into your planning up front so you don't miss a critical measure of impact when you implement. For example, when you design leadership development programs for underrepresented talent, you might want to create a pre- and post-survey that includes an assessment of leadership skills to see whether they've improved as a result of the program. You may also want to understand participants' career goals and track whether they are able to achieve them over the next year or more. These are great indicators of program success.

Be sure to integrate your metrics into existing people and business planning cadences rather than showing up a month after the plans and budgets are locked and attempting to influence plans then. Do you know that saying about not trying to teach a pig to sing because it wastes your time and it annoys the pig? My colleague Janelle is fond of saying that you don't want to be the person trying to teach the pig, or in this case, trying to wedge in DEIB metrics outside normal planning cycles. Understand the larger people-planning cadences, and piggyback (pun intended!) onto that process instead.

As your organizational efforts get more advanced, you could also look at adding more diversity dimensions, such as age. Looking at the intersectionality of gender and race in the United States can help you further pinpoint areas for action around equity. According to Lean In, the pay gap between women and men is often worse for women of color.[2] In many organizations, you may feel your representation of women is high overall, but when you layer in race and/or ethnicity and look at how many Black or Latina women are in software engineering roles, you may have only a handful.

Where possible and appropriate, disaggregate your data. For example, LGBTQ+ as a category covers both sexual orientation and gender identity. However, people who identify as transgendered face very different issues than those who identify as lesbian or gay. Understanding how these differences intersect with race and/or ethnicity can reveal gaps that need to be addressed that you would not necessarily see in aggregate.

Some aspects, such as disability and veteran status, are trickier to measure because there is no legal requirement to track these dimensions for many companies. And you need to be mindful that different countries have different laws governing the collection of diversity-related data. Successfully getting employees to self-identify can be very challenging if they face repercussions in their countries for how they identify or they feel the information will be used against them somehow. One other possibility is to sample the employee population, but that's only useful at very high levels, and it is less actionable.

You also have to involve many key stakeholders in measuring and being accountable to progress. Your first stop should be *business leadership*. Some parts of DEIB work are grassroots. This is not one of them. If DEIB goals and metrics are not already companywide, find senior leaders who are already sharing their objectives and key results in this area or who are open to it. Ideally, your CEO and executive staff are role modeling this. Next, make sure your HR leadership is on board. To be successful, you'll need to put consistent pressure on both HR and the business around what you're trying to achieve and whether or not you're getting there. *HR information systems* (HRIS) *teams* and *HR business analytics teams* are your best friends in this endeavor.

Ideally, DEIB metrics will be folded into the regular people analytics that are provided to business leaders. Lean on this team to design consumable visualizations that are also in line with other people analytics reports. Adding select employee engagement data to a DEIB scorecard is helpful to get another lens on the organization. You can create an index from questions about transparency, belonging, fairness, and more. Remember that it is employee sentiment, so work with your employee engagement colleagues to better understand what is most useful to highlight to senior leaders at your company. *HR business partners* and *site leaders* are the people on the front line of questions from the business. Try to engage them early so as not to surprise them.

Finally, your compensation, talent management, and legal partners are helpful in providing data on pay equity, talent mobility, and keeping your risks of data leaks to a minimum. Pay equity in particular is a metric that is getting more and more scrutiny these days. Colorado's Equal Pay for Equal Work Act went into effect January 1, 2021, and it requires employers with at least one employee in Colorado to share salaries for posted job opportunities based there and to post internal opportunities for promotion.[3] Several other states are considering enacting similar laws. According to a World at Work survey, 60 percent of companies are addressing pay equity in some way.[4] It makes me wonder what the other 40 percent of companies are thinking, but this statistic highlights how important equitable compensation is to demonstrating companies' commitment to DEIB.

And pay equity is closely related to talent mobility. If underrepresented groups are not getting promotional opportunities, then they will continue to be behind in average pay versus the majority. Globally, women earn 23 percent less than men on average, with workforce participation and access to credit being contributing factors, and it will take 257 years to close this economic gap at the rate we are currently going.[5]

Occasionally, you may run into executives who don't want to look at pay equity, inclusion sentiment, or talent mobility because they believe that when you look for a problem, you'll usually find one, so it's better not to look. Obviously, I don't subscribe to that mentality so when I do encounter this attitude, I just ask if that's how they run their business operations. Anyone who answers yes to that question probably isn't going to be in business much longer. Transparency around your goals and metrics for progress with both employees and customers can be scary, but it will help you build the trust and accountability needed to create a workplace culture of real inclusion.

## Some Lessons Learned

Janelle, the senior diversity leader I mentioned earlier, has been doing this work for almost a decade, and during that time she has learned a few lessons that may be helpful to you.

First, focus the conversation. It's OK to remove data that may create a distraction from the story you're trying to tell. In the companies she has worked with, she would usually have a handful of people at a supervisory level, with a majority of workers managed by these first-line managers. There was broad over- or underrepresentation of some demographics in the supervisor ranks because there were so few people in that level. As a result, Janelle did not include that data in her DEIB report to leaders so it wouldn't skew their perception of where the real issues were.

Second, recognize that not everyone will see the data the way you see it. The thing about metrics is, everyone wants more. And they want to know why the data is showing what it's showing, and many never focus on the most obvious thing. One time, Janelle had a discussion with a white woman business leader where they were talking about ethnicity and/or race representation in the organization. The leader couldn't get over the fact that white women were a percentage point lower in representation at the manager level than at the more junior level, despite the fact that they made up a higher percentage at the executive level. So they spun in their conversation for at least 10 minutes going back and forth trying to figure out what was going on behind the data and how they should fix it. However, Janelle felt that the bigger issue to tackle was the lack of women of color across all of their job levels and they were missing an opportunity by not focusing on it.

Ultimately, the conversation didn't go anywhere, and no action ended up being taken. Janelle had to decide to focus on other teams and issues that were more pressing instead. Looking back, she said she would have handled that conversation very differently. She would have talked about needing to look beyond your own issues to focus on the bigger picture and not centering your own experiences as the most important to address. The conversation taught her that it's important to set a baseline expectation when you begin these conversations around what you're going to review and what outcome you're driving toward to help keep it on track.

Lastly, anchor metrics to where you can actually drive action. One of my favorite sayings from Janelle is about using data "to admire the problem rather than using it to drive action." I couldn't agree more. In some conversations she's had, people have said they didn't believe the data because they looked around them and felt like they saw diversity that was not reflected in the data.

Engineering teams in particular feel like they can't solve DEIB problems without more data to determine the right actions to take. They want to get to the root cause and attack the issue from that vantage point. They will point out that it really seems like the issue of so few women choosing to go into engineering starts in high school where we see girls start to self-select out of the technical track. They then ask why we aren't tackling high school programs to increase the number of girls entering science, technology, engineering, and math (STEM) majors in college. Which is absolutely the right way to solve the problem.

But when we don't have the resources to tackle the high school pipeline and we do have people in the company under our responsibility who can be directly affected in their technical careers by our support, or lack thereof, it behooves us to start here, within our own organization.

I think this is my favorite lesson learned from Janelle on measuring success and how to take the appropriate actions. Focus on what the data tells you, define what's within your sphere of control, and take actions that will have a material and positive impact.

## PUTTING IT INTO ACTION

Review the list in Table 7.1 of potential metrics for success. Place a check next to the ones you are tracking today and which ones you plan to track in the future.

- What gaps do you see?

- Why do those gaps exist?

- How will you close those gaps?

### Table 7.1 **Tracking Metrics**

| Metric | Tracking Today? | Future? |
|---|---|---|
| Representation | | |
| Hiring funnel | | |
| Attrition rates | | |

| Metric | Tracking Today? | Future? |
|---|---|---|
| Onboarding surveys | | |
| Manager effectiveness assessments | | |
| Leadership development participation | | |
| Internal mobility | | |
| Succession plan slates | | |
| Performance ratings distribution | | |
| Promotion rates | | |
| Employee engagement or DEIB climate surveys | | |
| Pay equity | | |
| Employee relations issues | | |
| Exit surveys | | |
| Historical trends | | |
| Gap to market availability | | |
| Gap to customer demographics | | |
| Additional metrics? | | |

# WHO WILL MEASURE SUCCESS?

We've focused a lot on the what and how of measuring success. But who is accountable to doing the measuring and having the hard DEIB conversations with leaders on what to do next? Whether you're a company with a hundred people or a hundred thousand people, it will be worth investing in a DEIB team and structure that will allow you to achieve the results you are trying to measure.

Some initial questions you'll want to wrestle with are, do you hire someone with some deeper expertise in DEIB to support you, or do you lead it yourself? If you are the CEO of the company, the best thing you can do is lead it yourself. At Nielsen, the media ratings company, CEO David Kenny took on the title of chief diversity officer (CDO) in 2019 to ensure that it was a company priority. He said, "There is no more powerful position than the CEO, and, quite honestly, this isn't going to change if the people with power don't use that power to change it."[6]

To me, this is transformational thinking, and while many CEOs may unofficially do this, more CEOs need to take on the official mantle of CDO because it signals to underrepresented groups in the workplace that this truly is a priority and accountability on it both starts and stops with you. I have been privileged enough to work with several CEOs who have been very vocal about their role in supporting DEIB at the company and what they expect of all employees as a result. More than anything else, this tends to accelerate progress.

If you or your company isn't quite at the point of integrating the CEO role with the CDO, then the next best thing is to have a chief diversity officer reporting directly into the CEO. When the CDO is on the same playing field as other leaders at the company, that person cannot be ignored or pushed aside. It means the CDO perspective is taken as seriously as everyone else's at the leadership table.

And being in the center of discussions about business strategy and product development and people engagement means the CDO can insert a DEIB lens into the most impactful decisions for the company. If we truly believe in DEIB as a source of innovation and business growth, and we know that this role needs to work cross-functionally across all aspects of the four *P*s of the Inclusion Ecosystem, then we need to also position it that way in our organizational structure.

Unfortunately, the majority of companies see their DEIB functions as primarily *people* focused in the ecosystem, and they therefore put it under the umbrella of human resources. There are some companies now that combine the CDO role with their chief people officer (CPO) role. Companies as varied as Zendesk, Farmers Insurance, and Papa John's International have chief people and diversity officers (CPDOs) in place.

In my own career, all of my DEIB roles have been under the purview of human resources. Would I have preferred this to be different? Yes. Did it stop me from influencing the broader ecosystem anyway? No. But it's just one additional hurdle that doesn't need to be there on a road that is already littered with obstacles. So if you want to do this work more effectively and efficiently in the future, start by putting the DEIB responsibility outside HR. Wherever I go now in my career, I am very clear that DEIB work cuts across all functions of the company, and I expect to be supported in breaking down those boundaries and integrating all of our functions into an overarching DEIB strategy for the company as a whole, not just for talent.

Once you've established who's responsible for DEIB in your company, it's time to build a team dedicated to helping drive it. What do you look for? Having passion for social justice is necessary but not enough. If it isn't clear by now, the definition of a DEIB leader is no different than that of a great leader. To be a great leader, you have to be able to inspire people to follow you. You have to know how to get things done through others. And you have to effectively balance competing priorities.

In addition to that, being in DEIB specifically means you must be capable of empathizing with other lived experiences that are very different from your own. You also have to know how to act as a bridge between different points of view so that you can get folks aligned enough to make change happen. None of these skill sets are unique to a particular industry or education. The types of backgrounds that DEIB practitioners bring is hugely varied. You will see academics, lawyers, social workers, marketers, community organizers, consultants, activists, and businesspeople in this field. I've found that as long as someone has the capabilities mentioned earlier, it doesn't matter what background or experience they have. They have the potential to do this job really well.

What's important is that you practice what you preach as you build your DEIB team. You have to cast as wide a net as possible and apply all the concepts you've been teaching to others across the organization. Like any hiring manager, I've been tempted to cut corners and hire the people I've already worked with who I know could do the job well.

Given that these are DEIB roles, I have the advantage of there being no shortage of applicants from underrepresented backgrounds. But I give a lot of thought to the demographics of my team, and I am very intentional about balancing expertise and experience with different backgrounds and perspectives to create a whole team that is greater than the sum of each of its parts.

How you organize your DEIB team will depend on your organization and its needs. Most DEIB roles will fall into one of two buckets: business consulting or program management. On the business consulting side, *DEIB business partners* act as advisors to leaders on their team's assessments, communications, strategic action plans, and program implementations. On the program management side, *DEIB managers* are responsible for designing, developing, and executing DEIB-focused programs like employee resource groups, underrepresented group (URG) leadership development, or URG hiring partnerships.

If your organization is large enough, you may also hire DEIB roles focused on communications, analytics, suppliers, accessibility, learning, or recruiting, among others. If you are in a smaller company, your DEIB team often has to negotiate with these other functions to ensure that they have people focused on supporting DEIB efforts in their respective areas.

This is critical to do because if you don't own these areas yourself and you can't get what you need from other functions, then your DEIB efforts will be doomed to fail. I was working with a team whose business leaders were extremely motivated to make a difference in reducing attrition of underrepresented groups from their organization and had paid a significant amount of money to deploy an inclusion learning and diagnostics platform to help them pinpoint which teams were having inclusion issues so that we could target interventions more effectively.

Unfortunately, the platform never got launched because we could not get it prioritized for the technology support that was needed to implement it. This was one of the more painful experiences I've had because it wasn't just a sunk cost in terms of the dollars but also in terms of the time and energy wasted in dozens of conversations trying to get things moving forward and feeling roadblocked at every turn. But the key lesson I learned from this experience was that you've got to secure leadership support for implementation before you sign that contract and spend the money.

## Organizing Diversity Councils

This previous example is where having a diversity council could have been extremely helpful. *Diversity councils* are a group of leaders from across the company whose primary role is to champion, inform, and monitor DEIB efforts. They can go by many names, including *task forces*, *steering committees*, and *advisory boards*, and responsibilities will shift depending on how your organization wants to define their scope.

But they can be critical allies in implementing your DEIB strategies. Some companies choose to have senior, influential leaders with decision-making powers be the primary members of their council. Others prefer having leaders from all levels of the company participate to ensure more equitable representation and engagement.

Regardless of which way you go, it's imperative that the council have a clear purpose and defined role with real authority and influence across the organization. Otherwise, they tend to fall apart. In 1995, IBM helped to pioneer the concept of diversity councils by establishing eight *executive task forces*, each focused on a particular demographic, including people with disabilities, Black people, the LGBTQ+ community, and women. They made diversity a market-based issue, seeking ways to better understand and reach more diverse customers. And they were populated by senior managers, led by two executive cochairs, and supported by an executive sponsor who sat on their management committee.[7]

Their input helped IBM establish a market development organization focused on increasing the market of multicultural and women-owned businesses in the United States, which increased annual revenue by 30 times over just 3 years, and a focus on accessible products, which was projected to produce over a billion dollars in revenue over a 5- to 10-year period.[8] Since then, these task forces have evolved into *global and US constituency councils* that serve as ongoing guides to their diversity structure and priorities today.

## It Takes More Than Passion

When a friend of mine started as the head of DEIB at a biotechnology company, there was already an active DEIB working group. As is quite common, the group was full of people with passion but lacking in strategic subject matter expertise. She discovered that representation inside the working group was very skewed toward two particular departments.

The main reason this was a "problem" was that the group was having conversations and making recommendations that would affect the entire company, not just those two departments. Because job functions, working norms, and demographic representation varied widely from team to team, the DEIB working group's lack of understanding of these differences across the company was going to prevent them from engaging in the most effective actions and the most meaningful conversations.

So she knew she had to evolve the working group's membership to be more representative of the broader company. But she had to make sure the current members still felt valued and continued their participation. She wanted to invite people who had shown some level of interest in something related to DEIB or company culture, such as people who had attended a DEIB training or had joined their DEIB Slack channel, but had yet to attend a working group session.

These were the employees she felt were most likely to commit to joining the group because some level of DEIB interest already existed. She determined that it would be best for the DEIB team to create and drive the working group strategy. But to keep the working group engaged, she asked for feedback along the way from both existing and potential participants.

Her first attempt to expand the group's members was suggested by the working group itself. They attempted to diversify department representation by simply asking every attendee to invite someone new to the group, ideally from a department outside their own. They quickly learned that this didn't work because the employees didn't know a lot of people outside their own department. It actually skewed representation even more toward a single department.

As a result, she knew they needed to understand more about what was important to their internal stakeholders in order to meet their needs successfully. She spoke to people in various departments on what prevented them from attending the working group. Response themes centered around these:

- A lack of understanding of what attending a meeting was like, combined with feeling like they didn't know enough about DEIB to participate

- A lack of time to attend

- A lack of awareness the working group existed

Keeping all of these experiences in mind, she then designed the *liaison* role, which was new for the working group. She laid out exactly what to expect in a working group meeting, including such mundane details as the meeting flow and where to see the agenda. She also explicitly defined what was expected of liaisons—that they needed to attend the majority of meetings, bring their team's culture-related questions, and promote DEIB initiatives to their teams.

This reduced a lot of the nervousness that was holding some people back from participating. Perhaps most importantly, she made it very clear that no one in the group was expected to be a DEIB expert. She was clear that the working group was in fact a great place to start being exposed to various conversations in a safe learning space. And that it was expected for some of these conversations to be new topics for them to discuss. Employees could then sign up as interested, and a member of the DEIB team would meet with each person to answer any questions about meetings and expectations to build confidence before making an official commitment. This increased the chances that their first meeting would be a positive experience.

Because every department had their own "busy period," they also wanted to make the liaison commitment realistic given everyone's bandwidth constraints. The group would meet every other week for 30 to 60 minutes, and the liaison would be expected to attend the vast majority of meetings. However, the role was set for only six months and it could begin at any time. After the six months, the employee could opt to serve another six months, opt out, or help look for someone else on their team to rotate in.

Originally, they intended to make representation from every team required. However, due to some teams being stretched too thin at certain times of the year, combined with wanting to maintain a safe space where everyone who was there truly wanted to be there, they decided to make it optional. The role remained voluntary, but it qualified for a monetary spot award. They also understood that bandwidth changes, so there was no penalty for ending the position early beyond forfeiting the bonus. This flexibility led employees who were initially hesitant to join become much more comfortable stepping in.

They also realized that people couldn't attend something if they didn't hear about it beforehand. Despite promoting the DEIB working group as part of onboarding new employees and also promoting it on their DEIB Slack channel ahead of each of their meetings, some employees did not even know it existed. Reminding employees about the working group and liaison role on a quarterly basis via all-company channels has been helpful in attracting additional team representation.

With these tweaks, the program has been a notable success. They went from having 8 percent of company departments represented to having more than 40 percent represented in the first three months. Additionally, over 80 percent of the first wave of liaisons stayed on board for another rotation. They have made small adjustments over time to make it as easy as possible for liaisons to pass along information to their teams, but the structure of the role and commitment has stayed consistent.

As a result, they have been able to have conversations about companywide initiatives with far more points of view than before, and it has helped them have more successful program engagement in many areas. From feedback on which marketing strategy works best to reach their teams, to the common blockers of participation in programs of interest, this success has elevated their ability to support the broader organization's DEIB goals.

## Self-Care Is Not Optional

Successes like these are wonderful to see, but they are too few and far between. The reality for most people advocating for DEIB is lots of starts and stops, taking two steps forward but one step back, with slow progress somewhere along the way. In DEIB roles, you have to simultaneously be a therapist, coach, business strategist, program developer, teacher, and corporate conscience in the workplace, usually under conditions that mean you have no direct authority over decision-making.

There is so much emotional labor involved in driving change and dealing with some of the most polarizing and difficult issues in conversations that it takes a special kind of resiliency for anyone to remain engaged in driving this work over a long period of time. In every role I've held in this space, at some point I've always asked myself, "Is it time to quit?" because of the enormous energy I have had to expend to keep pushing for change in a way that leaders will embrace. There is no separating this work from my personal identity, and that takes a toll.

Which is why it's important for you to do two things as you embark on this journey. One, coach everyone you are enlisting in this work to take time out for self-care. For many people, engaging in this work can be traumatizing, and they need space to process their feelings and be able to address issues productively.

I recently had a conversation with a Black colleague who shared an experience that has been an all-too-common narrative within the Black community: a police officer looking for a suspected thief pulled a gun on my colleague in front of his own home without any evidence or provocation. He felt it was necessary to share this story with others who might not believe that racial profiling by the police happens, but you could tell that the retelling was retraumatizing him. So I had to tell him to take some time to process his emotions from that event and make sure that while he was trying to help others, he wasn't doing more harm to himself in the process.

Marginalized communities are often asked to educate others on their experiences, and that can be exhausting. We should always be mindful of what we are asking others to do as we work to further equity and justice, and we need to provide them the right support mechanisms to ensure that they are able to cope effectively.

Two, take time out to take care of yourself. If your energy reserves are depleted, it becomes much harder to coach and guide others in this work. Being an Asian woman, I have watched with more and more anxiety the alarming increase of anti-Asian violence incidents that have been happening since the COVID-19 pandemic was reported to have originated in China in late 2019.[9]

It is incredibly draining to support my family in modifying their routines out of fear that somebody could do them harm if we are not careful enough. I have told my elderly and frail parents not to walk outside in their neighborhood alone. I have asked them to tell me when they need something so that I can either order it delivered or pick it up for them.

My husband who is also Asian makes sure to drive his mother wherever she needs to go for errands or groceries. We've turned our worries into actions, which is one way to cope. I've also built in a self-care routine that involves exercise on a regular basis, watching lighthearted entertainment that takes my blood pressure down, and playing with my kids who ground me away from the work I do. I highly recommend professional coaches or therapy if you need it as well.

Surrounding yourself with a strong community of support you can lean on when you're doing DEIB work is really helpful. When I'm experiencing an issue or trying to solve a thorny problem, being able to reach out to peers at other companies and get their advice and resources has been invaluable to helping me maintain my equilibrium.

## COUNT EVERY WIN

Relatedly, make sure you take the time to recognize wins, even when they are small. We often spend so much time and effort trying to make big changes happen that when we see those smaller, incremental changes take place, it's easy to miss that those are wins too. And it's so important to realize that this is how progress most often takes place over time, through gradual change that shows up in small, 1 to 2 percent gains every year but that over time will add up to double-digit gains.

So reward yourself for the small wins, whether it's when you finally get that inclusive leadership training rolled out, or increase your self-identification rate for different diversity dimensions by 10 percent, or launch that partnership that brings in client revenue you can track directly to your DEIB efforts. And make sure you recognize key folks who were involved in those successes, whether that's through an annual DEIB award bestowed by the CEO or simple thank-you notes sent to an ERG leader's manager for supporting their work. I make it a point to add DEIB categories to every recognition program I can influence at companies as part of the strategy to highlight not just the work that's happened but also who's doing it. When teams spontaneously add their own Diversity Champion category to their recognition programs, I know we've gained traction.

It all matters and should be celebrated. Not only that, it should be communicated because it's not just about keeping yourself motivated but also about keeping everyone else who is putting their blood, sweat, and tears into DEIB motivated as well. Few things are more rewarding than seeing progress being made to prompt people to continue doing more. In one company, I created a one-page summary of all the initiatives we undertook in the previous year and what progress we made, which we then circulated with both our employees and clients. Once it was out, the phrase I heard over and over again was, "I had no idea we were doing so much in DEIB!"

## PUTTING IT INTO ACTION

Structure your diversity council:

- What is the charter for the diversity council?
    - To be an advisory body, a decision maker on policy, implementation arm, or all of the above?

- Who will members be?
    - Who has the most influence in your organization to support the charter?
    - Who is most passionate about DEIB?
    - Do you have representation across all functions, job levels, geographies, and demographics?

- Who will chair?
    - Senior leaders?
    - The DEIB leader?

- How will decisions get made?
    - Majority vote?
    - Consensus?

- How often will you meet?
    - Once a quarter?
    - Monthly?

- Whom will the council be accountable to?
    - The C suite?
    - Employees?

## KEY TAKEAWAYS

1. Before you begin measuring success, make sure you've got the right systems and processes in place to do it.

2. Measuring diversity is about representation. Measuring equity, inclusion, and belonging is about understanding employee sentiment and experiences.

3. Ensure that someone is tasked with driving DEIB at your company, whether that's the CEO or a DEIB team.

4. Diversity councils can go by many names, but be clear on their charters and responsibilities to make them effective.

5. There is so much emotional labor that goes into DEIB work. Take care of yourself and others who are doing it to sustain success over time.

# CHAPTER 8

# What's Next?

The future of work is changing. Each successive generation is getting more and more diverse and bringing different expectations around DEIB to the workplace.[1] For millennials and generation Z, diversity and inclusion in the workplace are not nice-to-haves. They are need-to-haves. More younger professionals are prioritizing alignment with personal values in where they choose to work.[2] And for companies to remain competitive and attract these workers into their workforce, they must respond. Yet as of the first quarter 2020, only 39 percent of the Fortune 500 had a diversity executive with the title of "director" or higher on their roster.[3] What are the rest of y'all doing? Reading this book is a good start. Now turn it into action.

As renowned executive coach Marshall Goldsmith says, "What got you here won't get you there."[4] While many companies have become successful over time in spite of a lack of focus on DEIB, that does not mean their success will continue. Nor does it mean that they have reached the full potential of their success. Who knows what kind of success they would have been able to unlock had they had a more diverse workforce generating more innovation and expanding marketplaces in ways they cannot imagine today? Business leaders inherently know that they cannot become complacent in their business. Otherwise, the next startup or technology will disrupt and displace them. So why do we accept this in our human capital and DEIB practices?

## A HUMAN-CENTERED APPROACH

We have to experiment and iterate more in the field of DEIB. Many companies are applying a *design-thinking process* to this space. There are many models for design thinking out there, but they are all based on the human-centered design process developed by Hasso Plattner and David Kelley in 2004: empathize, work together, and fail effectively. I am partial to the Stanford d.school model, which I've adapted a bit in Figure 8.1 to apply more to DEIB practices.[5]

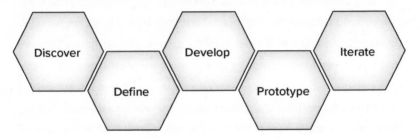

Figure 8.1 **Applying Design Thinking to DEIB**

According to Tim Brown, executive chair of IDEO, one of the premier design firms in the world, "Design thinking is a human-centered approach to innovation that draws from the designer's toolkit to integrate the needs of people, the possibilities of technology, and the requirements for business success."[6] When you apply a design-thinking process, you are approaching the problem of DEIB with a human-centered lens, where you are trying to discover and empathize with experiences very different from your own and define and develop solutions that may or may not work.

The beauty of the design-thinking process is that you experiment with prototypes and then you iterate based on what you learned. It gives you permission to fail at trying new things. This attitude of failing rapidly, learning from your mistakes, and making the changes you need to keep the cycle going is invaluable to DEIB work because it reduces the fear of not getting it right immediately. With design thinking, you remove the barrier to inaction. You invite many diverse voices and perspectives into the room. You take the time to understand those voices and perspectives deeply. And you bring together people from all walks of life to develop solutions that you could not have imagined on your own or within a more homogeneous group.

In this new age of social media instant gratification and judgment, companies can no longer afford to sit on the sidelines. They are now expected to make a positive difference in the world, on social and moral issues beyond what their business might focus on, by employees, customers, and shareholders alike. Being silent on DEIB-related issues is no longer interpreted as staying neutral. It's seen as not taking a stand for equality and justice. CEOs now have to be social activists, standing up for their people, in addition to their mission, values, and purpose.[7]

Tim Cook of Apple and Marc Benioff of Salesforce are great examples of CEOs who are very outspoken on human rights issues, and there are many more as calls for company statements on social issues have gained traction. As the country becomes more polarized ideologically and politically, and our legislative bodies get more and more gridlocked on controversial issues so that nothing seems to ever move forward, people are looking more often to business leaders to get things moving and fill the moral void.

Businesses are starting to respond by leveraging their power in support of DEIB. Goldman Sachs announced that they would serve as IPO underwriters for only those companies that had at least one underrepresented group on their board, with a focus on women.[8] Major League Baseball pulled its 2021 All-Star Game out of Georgia in response to the passing of voter suppression laws that disproportion-ately affected millions of Black voters in the state.[9]

It's no longer about "feel-good" initiatives designed to let you pat yourself on the back because you're doing something. It's about using your business leverage to incentivize positive change in support of equitable outcomes for all.

## COVID IS THE NEW NORMAL

The pandemic has also accelerated the future of work to be more flexible. The majority of businesses were forced into a remote-work experiment to curb the spread of the COVID-19 virus. This taught many companies that they could in fact support more flexible work arrange-ments for their employees without sacrificing business performance in exchange.

As more companies adopt remote working and flexible work schedules more permanently as we come out of the pandemic, it will also mean some DEIB issues will become heightened. How do you cre-ate inclusion and belonging when your employees are so scattered geo-graphically that they only get together in person one or two times per year? How do you maintain equitable practices across the company when different locations can result in different salary bands, different office amenities, and different levels of exposure to career paths and leadership opportunities? These are just some of the thorny issues that will need to be resolved as our workplaces and what working together really means in the next iteration of our remote workplaces.

We must also remember that there are a lot of pluses to DEIB work that will result out of the pandemic as well. Remote-working policies also mean companies can recruit from anywhere, not just local tal-ent pools, which could open up your recruiting pipelines to talent you may not have otherwise considered. More flexible working schedules can attract more women, new parents, and retirees to the workforce. Remote work also offers higher accessibility to people with disabilities who might have otherwise been shut out of roles that required long commutes or staying at a desk all day. Managers who now have to focus more on results than face time are learning how to overcome their biases and ensure more equitable treatment of all their team members. This new era is creating significant opportunities for DEIB to expand and advance.

## THE PRESSURE IS ON

Regulation is also changing the DEIB landscape. California passed a law requiring that public companies have at least one woman on their board of directors by 2019, and it required future increases in the number of women on their board that will be tied to the size of the board. They also passed a law in 2020 requiring at least one and up to three board members from underrepresented racial and/or ethnic communities, depending on board size.[10] Other states, including New Jersey, Massachusetts, and Washington, are following suit and introducing their own legislation requiring women representation on public company boards.

The Nasdaq recently proposed that companies listed on its exchange would be required to meet certain minimum diversity targets or explain in writing why they aren't doing so.[11] The House of Representatives Financial Services Committee on Diversity and Inclusion is considering bills that would require diversity data disclosures by all major banks doing business in the United States.[12] These are additional ways that the government is applying pressure on companies to better serve our more marginalized communities.

Shareholders are applying their own activist pressure as well. Since 2017, State Street has been calling on companies with previously no women on their boards to engage and add at least one female board member.[13] Since then, more than 860 publicly traded companies have done so, as mentioned earlier in Chapter 6. BlackRock plans to push companies for greater ethnic and gender diversity for their boards and workforce by voting against directors who fail to act in an effort to drive change.[14]

Shareholders make up a key stakeholder group that businesses must satisfy as they ramp up their DEIB efforts. Vanguard announced that beginning at their 2021 annual meetings, their funds may vote against directors at companies where progress on board diversity falls behind their peer companies and market expectations.[15]

These moves are part of a sea change in expectations around DEIB work. We are no longer satisfied with DEIB commitments that are not backed up with results that can be seen at the highest levels of an organization. And shareholders are recognizing that they have the power to hold businesses accountable to those results.

Employees and customers alike are demanding more from businesses. In the United States, 75 percent of workers believe they have the right to speak up against their employers.[16] When 20,000 Google employees staged a walkout in protest of extraordinary severance payments to executives accused of sexual harassment, Google ended its practice of forced arbitration as it relates to cases of discrimination.[17]

After Nike did an ad campaign featuring Colin Kaepernick, the football player who has been a controversial figure since kneeling during the national anthem at games to protest police brutality against the Black community, consumers either loved it or hated it. Some may have burned Nike products, but more bought them as Nike's sales increased by 31 percent, and their brand value increased by $6 billion a year later.[18]

We live in a world now where people recognize they don't just have to talk about an issue. They can act on them in ways that express their beliefs about DEIB, and they are exercising their right to do so.

All of this makes me hopeful for the future. I am hopeful that the level of activism across all fronts continues in support of more diversity, equity, inclusion, and belonging. And I am hopeful that with each successive generation of people and technology in the workplace, change will continue to accelerate as we recognize more and more that DEIB is not an option but, rather, an imperative in the workplace.

## CDO AS JACK-OF-ALL-TRADES

As a chief diversity officer, what I have also found is that my skill sets are not just focused on DEIB issues. More often than not, I have had to be a jack-of-all-trades in order to understand more aspects of our business operations and HR strategies than most people across the company.

You want to know where underrepresented applicants are falling out of the hiring pipeline? I first need to work with our applicant-tracking system experts to configure the system to actually track and output that data. Then I need to train the recruiters, interviewers, and hiring managers on what they need to do not only to ensure an inclusive hiring process but also to make sure they are inputting the data we need in the appropriate ways. Then I need to work with our analytics team to pull the data into digestible reports for our business leaders to review and act on.

You want our client events to be more inclusive of all attendees? Let me talk to our event registration website vendor about adding in fields for pronouns, dietary restrictions, and accommodations needs. The events team has to make sure there are different food options available, nursing rooms set up, sign language interpreters or live closed captioning, and/or braille on signage, among other things. Activities should be accessible to those with mobility issues, and we need to review our speaker lineup to ensure that diverse backgrounds are represented on stage.

I hope you can see from these examples that DEIB isn't some simple matter of training people on unconscious bias or about building more partnerships with diversity-focused organizations. It requires redesigning how the company operates, often from the ground up.

# ONE SIZE DOES NOT FIT ALL

As you embark on your DEIB imperative, it's important to understand that there is no one-size-fits-all solution to the issue of diversity, equity, inclusion, and belonging. What works at one company may not work at another. There is a complicated set of factors that can affect our ability to make progress.

Differences in industries, regulations, company sizes, geography, and cultures, to name a few, need to be taken into account as you are developing your strategies and solutions. For example, tech companies are very different from financial services companies. Where the tech company might have a philosophy of "move fast and break things," the financial services company might be much more "measure three times, cut once."

So you may be able to gather lots of data at the tech company to inform your actions, but maybe you have to build deep relationships inside the financial services company to get anything moving. It's important to understand what your organization's leaders value and how to work with them effectively.

Different cultures also have different definitions of what *diversity* means to them. In India, caste is a unique part of the diversity conversation. In Australia, you might focus on aboriginal or Indigenous peoples. In the Middle East, religious diversity might dominate. The people in every country will differ in their DEIB priorities, and if your company has operations outside the United States, you will need to build a framework that can be applied globally but implemented in locally relevant ways.

This means not taking what you do in the United States and implementing the same thing in Mexico. It means orienting everyone around the goal of DEIB but supporting them to translate that to meaningful action that is relevant to their culture. It can be particularly tempting to orient around a single commonality across the globe, like gender equity. I would encourage you to think more broadly than that because raising up one issue tends to make other groups feel left out, which is not inclusion.

What I've found to be more effective is allowing leaders within different countries to set their own DEIB goals and action plans that are accretive to your overarching global vision. At Yahoo!, I had partners responsible for DEIB initiatives in their regions, and they were given the autonomy to define local DEIB objectives and act on them, leveraging centralized resources when necessary and coordinating across other global sites when shared objectives meant we could amplify the impact.

A great example, as mentioned in Chapter 3, was when our women's ERG led a companywide, global career development event. With input from our global sites, they decided to plan a monthlong series of events, with some broadcast and recorded virtual talks showcasing our global leaders. The event also included some site-specific activities developed and implemented by the local leadership ranging from internal one-to-one mentorship with leaders to external speaker panels. It was a huge success with over half the company's women participating in at least one event.

When you're dealing with different cultures and customs around the globe, you will inevitably encounter challenging questions and issues for which there is no easy resolution. A DEIB colleague gave an example that would surely be faced by transportation companies that operate worldwide: what to do if a male driver whose religious beliefs forbade him from being alone with a woman who was not his wife, which meant he would refuse to pick up women to transport them to their destinations? What value takes precedence in such a case: his right to practice his religion or women's rights for equal access to services? Issues like this must be worked through with care and input from local leaders on how to best uphold the company's values as well as respecting local values that may be in opposition to each other.

Company size can also make a big difference to how DEIB initiatives get deployed. When you are a small startup, you have the opportunity to build DEIB into the company's DNA from the ground up. It's actually the best time to have a focus on DEIB as you are building the culture and setting the tone and vision for what the company will grow to become. Executives at Lever, a recruiting technology platform company, started thinking about DEIB from their very beginnings, convening a diversity and inclusion task force when they were just 10 employees. And that intentionality paid off with a gender-balanced workforce: 53 percent of their managers and 40 percent of their board members were female, and 40 percent of their workforce was nonwhite as of January 2017.[19]

For organizations that are growing rapidly, it can be incredibly chaotic, and having structured talent processes may seem like a pipe dream. What's key is to implement what you can inside of your business context. Don't have a performance review process? At least ask managers to gather 360-degree input on their employees to add multiple perspectives to help mitigate managers' bias. No time or money to invest in leadership development? Look at your leadership role models in the company, and ask them to mentor some of your high-potential underrepresented talent. Trying to hire more women? Offer flexible working arrangements and emphasize results, not a 9-to-5 schedule. Remember, every small change in experience you make contributes to a bigger equity and inclusion outcome.

Many small businesses aren't on a hypergrowth curve though. When your organization is small and stable or growing at a more measured pace, you may not have as much opportunity to change your demographic ratios through hiring. In which case, focusing on inclusion, equity, and belonging becomes even more important to your efforts. Celebrate holidays and events that are not United States centric, create a DEIB award for employees, and host learning or community events focused on different DEIB issues. Those are all ways to support a more inclusive culture and signal your company's strong commitment to DEIB. Make sure you engage in an inclusive hiring process for each new role you hire as you have fewer opportunities to leverage to bring more diversity into your firm. Ensuring that you create listening sessions to surface issues and involve your employees in brainstorming and implementing solutions will go far toward supporting your DEIB commitment.

While larger companies have the resources to dedicate to hiring full-time DEIB staff, it's not 100 percent necessary to do it. While it can be a game changer to have employees fully dedicated to closing the DEIB gaps at your company, it's really up to the leadership to drive the transformation and set the tone from the top. So even if you don't have the resources or infrastructure to do all of the full-blown strategies provided in this book, you can still apply the same principles of CARE and the four Ps to this work and come up with a plan that you can execute. In fact, many of the strategies in this book don't require much in terms of resources or people. What they do require is follow-through on your DEIB commitment and the willingness to change your own status quo.

No matter what kind of organization you are running, it's important to adapt. DEIB is a constantly changing field involving flawed and emotional human beings who don't always behave rationally. There is no perfection in this work, only failure and progress. What matters is that we are constantly experimenting and trying and learning and pushing the envelope. And as we learn more about what works and what doesn't, I am hopeful that we will begin to achieve our vision of a workplace culture of inclusion that delivers real results.

# Glossary

**accessibility:** The design of products or environments that allows them to be used effectively by people with disabilities.

**accommodation:** A modification or adjustment of a job, process, or work environment to enable people with disabilities to perform tasks to the same extent as people without disabilities.

**affirmative action:** An active effort to improve employment or educational opportunities for members of minority groups and for women in the United States.

**ally:** Someone who uses their power or privilege to support and protect those who do not have the same power or privilege.

**belonging:** A sense of connection to a group, where you feel you are accepted and important.

**bias:** A tendency or inclination toward or away from something or someone.

**BIPOC:** Black, Indigenous, and people of color.

**Black Lives Matter:** A global movement protesting violence and police brutality against the Black community.

**cisgender:** Describes someone whose sense of identity and gender correspond to their birth sex.

**cultural appropriation:** The adoption of aspects of a culture or identity by another culture or identity in a way that is disrespectful or profiteering.

**disability:** A physical or mental impairment or medical condition that substantially limits a major life activity.

**disparate or adverse impact:** When policies, practices, or systems that are intended to be neutral actually have a disproportionate impact on a minoritized group.

**diversity:** All the differences and similarities that make each person unique. Often refers to demographic representation in the context of the workplace.

**employee resource groups (ERGs):** Supportive communities inside workplaces that form around a common characteristic or experience.

**equality:** Everyone getting the same fair treatment in terms of opportunities, access, and resources.

**equity:** Giving everyone what they need to succeed in the workplace.

**ethnicity:** Belonging to a social group that has a common national or cultural tradition.

**first generation:** Born to immigrant parents.

**gender identity:** A personal perception of one's own gender.

**HBCUs:** Historically Black colleges and universities.

**HSIs:** Hispanic serving institutions.

**imposter syndrome:** Not believing you are as competent as other people perceive you to be.

**inclusion:** Leveraging the diversity within an organization to its fullest potential.

**Indigenous:** People who are native to a land or place.

**intersectionality:** Recognizing that different social identities can overlap—for example, women of color.

**LGBTQ+:** Lesbian, gay, bisexual, transgender, queer, and more.

**marginalized:** To be treated as peripheral or unimportant within society.

**MeToo:** A social movement against sexual abuse and harassment.

**microaggression:** A comment or action that subtly communicates a bias against a particular group.

**military:** The armed forces.

**minority:** A culturally, ethnically, or racially distinct group that coexists with but is subordinate to a more dominant group.

**neurodivergent:** When someone's brain works differently than what is considered typical or the norm.

**nonbinary:** Someone who does not conform to the idea that only two genders, male and female, exist.

**prejudice:** An assumption or opinion about someone based on their perceived membership to a particular group.

**privilege:** An advantage that other people don't have.

**queer:** An umbrella term for someone who identifies outside of the cisgender, heterosexual majority.

**race:** A group sharing outward physical characteristics and some commonalities of culture and history.

**stereotype:** A generalized belief about people who have a particular characteristic that is often untrue or unfair.

**transgender:** Having a gender identity or gender expression that differs from their birth sex.

**unconscious or implicit biases:** Social stereotypes about certain groups of people that individuals form outside their own conscious awareness.

**underrepresented group or talent (URG or URT):** A group that is proportionately less represented in relation to their broader population.

**universal design:** Planning and development of products and environments that are usable by as wide a range of people as possible.

**upstander:** Someone who actively intervenes against inappropriate behavior.

# Notes

## Chapter 1

1. *Encyclopaedia Britannica*, "Affirmative Action: Definition, History, & Cases," accessed June 1, 2021, https://www.britannica.com/topic/affirmative-action.

2. Adapted from Lee Gardenswartz and Anita Rowe, *Diverse Teams at Work*, 2d ed. (Alexandria, VA: SHRM, 2003); and Lee Gardenswartz, Anita Rowe, Patricia Digh, and Martin Bennett, *The Global Diversity Desk Reference* (San Francisco: Pfeiffer, 2003). Internal Dimensions and External Dimensions are adapted from Marilyn Loden and Judy Rosener, *Workplace America!* (Homewood, IL: Business One Irwin, 1991).

3. Laura Sherbin and Ripa Rashid, "Diversity Doesn't Stick Without Inclusion," *Harvard Business Review*, February 1, 2017, https://hbr.org/2017/02/diversity -doesnt-stick-without-inclusion.

4. Harvard Office for Diversity, Inclusion & Belonging, *DIB Glossary: Foundational Concepts & Affirming Language*, accessed June 26, 2021, https://dib .harvard.edu/dib-glossary.

5. Indeed: Job Search, accessed June 26, 2021, https://www.indeed.com/jobs? q=Title%3A%28inclusion+Diversity%29&l=San+Francisco%2C+CA&rad ius=50.

6. Bruce Anderson, "Why the Head of Diversity Is the Job of the Moment," LinkedIn, September 2, 2020, https://business.linkedin.com/talent -solutions/blog/diversity/2020/why-the-head-of-diversity-is-the-job-of -the-moment.

7. Richi Zweigenhaft, "Fortune 500 CEOs, 2000–2020: Still Male, Still White," *Society Pages*, October 28, 2020, https://thesocietypages.org/specials/fortune-500 -ceos-2000-2020-still-male-still-white/.

8. Grant Thornton, *Women in Business: Building a Blueprint for Action*, March 2019, https://www.grantthornton.global/en/insights/women-in-business -2019/women-in-business-report-2019/.

9. Jacob Poushter and Nicholas Kent, *The Global Divide on Homosexuality Persists*, Pew Research Center, June 25, 2020, https://www.pewresearch.org/global /2020/06/25/global-divide-on-homosexuality-persists/.

10. United Nations Department of Economic and Social Affairs, *Disability and Employment*, accessed February 2, 2021, https://www.un.org/development /desa/disabilities/resources/factsheet-on-persons-with-disabilities /disability-and-employment.html.

11. Cary Funk and Kim Parker, *Diversity in the STEM Workforce Varies Widely Across Jobs*, Pew Research Center, January 9, 2018, https://www.pewsocial trends.org/2018/01/09/diversity-in-the-stem-workforce-varies-widely -across-jobs/.

12. Simon Sinek, *Start with Why: How Great Leaders Inspire Everyone to Take Action* (Harlow, England: Penguin Books, 2011).

13. Vivian Hunt, Dennis Layton, and Sara Prince, "Why Diversity Matters," McKinsey & Company, January 2015, https://www.mckinsey.com/business -functions/organization/our-insights/why-diversity-matters#.

14. Josh Bersin, "Why Diversity and Inclusion Has Become a Business Priority," Josh Bersin, December 7, 2015, https://joshbersin.com/2015/12/why-diversity -and-inclusion-will-be-a-top-priority-for-2016/.

15. Corporate Leadership Council, Corporate Executive Board, *Creating Competitive Advantage Through Workforce Diversity*, Gartner, 2012, https:// s3.amazonaws.com/texassports_com/documents/2014/11/24/corporate _leadership_council_report.pdf.

16. Sylvia Ann Hewlett, Melinda Marshall, and Laura Sherbin, "How Diversity Can Drive Innovation," *Harvard Business Review*, December 2013, https:// hbr.org/2013/12/how-diversity-can-drive-innovation.

17. Pooneh Baghai, Olivia Howard, Lakshmi Prakash, and Jill Zucker, "Women as the Next Wave of Growth in US Wealth Management," McKinsey & Company, July 29, 2020, https://www.mckinsey.com/industries /financial-services/our-insights/women-as-the-next-wave-of-growth-in -us-wealth-management.

18. Elizabeth Weise and Jessica Guynn, "Black and Hispanic Computer Scientists Have Degrees from Top Universities, but Don't Get Hired in Tech," *USA TODAY*, October 12, 2014, https://www.usatoday.com/story/tech/2014 /10/12/silicon-valley-diversity-tech-hiring-computer-science-graduates -african-american-hispanic/14684211.

19. Leila Janah (@Leila_c), "Talent is equally distributed, but opportunity is not," Twitter, August 25, 2018, https://twitter.com/leila_c/status/10333544 70682451970?lang=en.

20. Prison Policy Initiative, "U.S. Incarceration Rates by Race and Ethnicity, 2010," accessed February 4, 2021, https://www.prisonpolicy.org/graphs /raceinc.html.

21. Marlette Jackson and Paria Rajai, "Does Your Definition of Leadership Exclude Women of Color?," *Harvard Business Review*, January 20, 2021, https://hbr .org/2021/01/does-your-definition-of-leadership-exclude-women-of-color.

22. Claire Cain Miller, Kevin Quealy, and Margot Sanger Katz, "The Top Jobs Where Women Were Outnumbered by Men Named John," *New York Times*, April 24, 2018, https://www.nytimes.com/interactive/2018/04/24/upshot /women-and-men-named-john.html.

23. Samantha McLaren, "How GoDaddy Increased Diversity at Every Level by Transforming Its Employee Evaluations," LinkedIn, November 6, 2017, https://business.linkedin.com/talent-solutions/blog/diversity/2017/how -godaddy-increased-diversity-at-every-level-by-transforming-its-employee -evaluations.

24. Mind Tools, "The Action Priority Matrix," MindTools, accessed June 27, 2021, https://www.mindtools.com/pages/article/newHTE_95.htm #:~:text=The%20Action%20Priority%20Matrix%20is,Quick%20wins .&text=The%20Action%20Priority%20Matrix%20is,Quick%20wins.

## Chapter 2

1. Jennifer Robison, "Turning Around Employee Turnover," Gallup, May 8, 2008, https://news.gallup.com/businessjournal/106912/turning-around -your-turnover-problem.aspx.

2. Sarah Greenberg, "Defining Executive Presence: Why Women Deserve a Customized Approach to Leadership Development," *Forbes*, April 16, 2020, https://www.forbes.com/sites/forbescoachescouncil/2020/04/16/defining -executive-presence-why-women-deserve-a-customized-approach-to -leadership-development/?sh=1f380dc16003.

3. Mattel, "Barbie Launches a New Line of Black Dolls Called So In Style," September 29, 2009, https://investors.mattel.com/news-releases/news -release-details/barbier-launches-new-line-black-dolls-called-so-style153.

4. Forbes Insights, *Fostering Innovation Through a Diverse Workforce*, accessed June 26, 2021, https://images.forbes.com/forbesinsights/StudyPDFs /Innovation_Through_Diversity.pdf.

5. Mallory Simon, "HP Looking into Claim Webcams Can't See Black People," CNN, December 23, 2009, http://www.cnn.com/2009/TECH/12/22 /hp.webcams/index.html.

6. Subhod Mishra, "ESG Matters," Harvard Law School Forum on Corporate Governance, January 14, 2020, https://corpgov.law.harvard .edu/2020/01/14/esg-matters/#:~:text=Higher%20ESG%20Associated%20 with%20Higher,%2C%20EVA%20Spread%2C%20and%20ROIC .&text=Thus%2C%20high%20ESG%20companies%20are,is%20also%20 correlated%20with%20volatility.

7. Salesforce, "About Us: Pledge 1%," accessed March 7, 2021, https://www .salesforce.org/pledge-1/.

8. David Hessekiel, "The Rise and Fall of the Buy-One-Give-One Model at TOMS," *Forbes*, April 28, 2021, https://www.forbes.com/sites/davidhessekiel

/2021/04/28/the-rise-and-fall-of-the-buy-one-give-one-model-at-toms /?sh=33d8fd4971c4.

9. Nike, "Our Black Community Commitment," accessed June 26, 2021, https://purpose.nike.com/our-commitment-to-the-black-community.

10. *New York Times*, "How George Floyd Died, and What Happened Next," May 25, 2021, https://www.nytimes.com/article/george-floyd.html.

11. GLAAD, "FAQ: Prop 8," accessed May 30, 2021, https://www.glaad.org /marriage/prop8.

12. Kyle VanHemert, "The Tech Companies That Helped Fight Proposition 8," *Gizmodo*, August 4, 2010, https://gizmodo.com/the-tech-companies-that -helped-fight-proposition-8-5604749; and Chris Cadelago, "Levi Strauss & Company Joins Campaign to Defeat Prop 8," *SFGate*, October 7, 2008, https://blog.sfgate.com/chronstyle/2008/10/07/levi-strauss-company -joins-campaign-to-defeat-prop-8/.

13. Kate Rooney and Yasmin Khorram, "Tech Companies Say They Value Diversity, but Reports Show Little Change in Last Six Years," CNBC, June 12, 2020, https://www.cnbc.com/2020/06/12/six-years-into-diversity-reports-big -tech-has-made-little-progress.html.

14. Bernadette Dillon and Juliet Bourke, *The Six Signature Traits of Inclusive Leadership* (Deloitte University Press, 2016), https://www2.deloitte.com /content/dam/Deloitte/au/Documents/human-capital/deloitte-au-hc-six -signature-traits-inclusive-leadership-020516.pdf.

15. Emily Glazer and Theo Francis, "CEO Pay Increasingly Tied to Diversity Goals," *Wall Street Journal*, June 2, 2021, https://www.wsj.com/articles /ceos-pledged-to-increase-diversity-now-boards-are-holding-them -to-it-11622626380.

16. Morgan Fecto, "Uber Sets Diversity Goals, Ties Executive Compensation to D&I Success," HR Dive, July 17, 2019, https://www.hrdive.com/news/uber -sets-diversity-goals-ties-executive-compensation-to-di-success/558935/.

17. Jingcong Zhao, "These Companies Are Tying Executive Bonuses to Diversity Goals," PayScale, March 7, 2019, https://www.payscale.com/compensation -today/2019/03/tie-bonuses-to-diversity-goals.

18. Frank Dobbin and Alexandra Kalev, "Why Diversity Programs Fail," *Harvard Business Review*, July-August 2016, https://hbr.org/2016/07/why-diversity -programs-fail.

19. Peter Economy, "How the Platinum Rule Trumps the Golden Rule Every Time," *Inc.*, March 17, 2016, https://www.inc.com/peter-economy/how -the-platinum-rule-trumps-the-golden-rule-every-time.html.

## Chapter 3

1. Ivana Saric, "U.S. Women Won't Reach Pay Equity with Men for at Least 60 Years," Axios, March 30, 2021, https://www.axios.com/wef-gender-equality -2021-e7e074e0-baa0-4c89-935a-1a5107b2a2c1.html.

2. Prosci, "The Prosci ADKAR Model," accessed July 2, 2021, https://www.prosci
.com/adkar.

3. Tom Nolan, "The No. 1 Employee Benefit That No One's Talking About,"
Gallup Workplace, accessed May 23, 2021, https://www.gallup.com/work
place/232955/no-employee-benefit-no-one-talking.aspx#:~:text=People
%20leave%20managers%2C%20not%20companies.&text=One%20in%
20two%20employees%20have,of%20the%20American%20Manager%20
report.

4. Daniel Coyle, *The Talent Code* (London: Arrow Books. 2010).

**Chapter 4**

1. Lean In, "The Broken Rung is the Biggest Obstacle Women Face," accessed July
10, 2021, https://leanin.org/women-in-the-workplace-2019#!; and Samantha
Kubota, "What Is the Bamboo Ceiling? Here's What Asian Americans Want
You to Know," *TODAY* show, March 17, 2021, https://www.today.com/tmrw
/what-bamboo-ceiling-here-s-what-asian-americans-want-you-t212014.

2. Tara Sophia Mohr, "Why Women Don't Apply for Jobs Unless They're 100%
Qualified," *Harvard Business Review*, August 25, 2014, https://hbr.org/2014
/08/why-women-dont-apply-for-jobs-unless-theyre-100-qualified.

3. Bill Chappell, "Sexist Reactions to an Ad Spark #ILookLikeAnEngineer
Campaign," NPR, August 4, 2015, https://www.npr.org/sections/thetwo
-way/2015/08/04/429362127/sexist-reactions-to-an-ad-spark-ilooklikean
engineer-campaign.

4. Valentina Zarya, "Exclusive: Why GoDaddy Promoted 30% More Women
This Year," *Fortune*, October 2, 2017, https://fortune.com/2017/10/02
/godaddy-ceo-blake-irving-women/.

5. Paola Cecchi-Dimeglio, "How Gender Bias Corrupts Performance Reviews,
and What to Do About It," *Harvard Business Review*, April 12, 2017, https://
hbr.org/2017/04/how-gender-bias-corrupts-performance-reviews-and
-what-to-do-about-it.

6. Dan Harris, "What Are the Drivers of Employee Engagement, and Why Do
They Matter?," *Manager Mysteries & Mishaps Podcast*, Quantum Workplace,
June 25, 2019, website, 18:47, https://www.quantumworkplace.com/podcast
/what-are-drivers-of-employee-engagement-and-why-do-they-matter.

7. Richard L. Zweigenhaft, "Diversity Among Fortune 500 CEOs from 2000 to
2020: White Women, Hi-Tech South Asians, and Economically Privileged
Multilingual Immigrants from Around the World," *Who Rules America?*,
January 2021, https://whorulesamerica.ucsc.edu/power/diversity_update
_2020.html.

8. Diversity Best Practices, "Linking ERG Roles to the Talent Development Process and Rewarding ERG Leaders," January 2021, https://seramount.com
/resources/research-report-linking-erg-roles-to-talent-development-process/.

9. Manichan Joy Nguyen, "Wells Fargo Diverse Leaders Program," *CEO Act!on for Diversity & Inclusion*, https://www.ceoaction.com/actions/wells-fargo-diverse-leaders-programs/.

10. Frank Dobbin and Alexandra Kalev, "Why Diversity Programs Fail," *Harvard Business Review*, July-August 2016, https://hbr.org/2016/07/why-diversity-programs-fail.

11. Herminia Ibarra and Nana von Bernuth, "Want More Diverse Senior Leadership? Sponsor Junior Talent," *Harvard Business Review*, October 9, 2020, https://hbr.org/2020/10/want-more-diverse-senior-leadership-sponsor-junior-talent.

12. Dobbin and Kalev, "Why Diversity Programs Fail."

13. David Rock and Heidi Grant Halvorson, "Is Your Company's Training Making You More Biased?," *Strategy + Business*, May 8, 2017, https://www.strategy-business.com/blog/Is-Your-Companys-Diversity-Training-Making-You-More-Biased.

14. Frank Dobbin and Alexandra Kalev, "Why Doesn't Diversity Training Work?," *Anthropology Now*, September 2018, https://scholar.harvard.edu/files/dobbin/files/an2018.pdf.

15. Allison Scott, Freada Klein Kapor, and Uriridiakoghene Onovakpuri, *Tech Leavers Study*, Kapor Center for Social Impact, 2017, https://mk0kaporcenter5ld71a.kinstacdn.com/wp-content/uploads/2017/08/TechLeavers2017.pdf.

16. Shep Hyken, "Starbucks Closes 8,000 Stores for Racial Bias Training—Is It Enough?," *Forbes*, June 1, 2018, https://www.forbes.com/sites/shephyken/2018/06/01/starbucks-closes-8000-stores-for-racial-bias-training-is-it-enough/?sh=192acd4c2831.

17. Project Implicit, accessed May 9, 2021, https://implicit.harvard.edu/implicit/.

## Chapter 5

1. Karen Catlin, *Better Allies: Everyday Actions to Create Inclusive, Engaging Workplaces* (Las Vegas: Better Allies Press, 2019).

2. Alex Allen, "The Cisco Customer Experience Journey to an Inclusive Culture: Leveraging the Power of Proximity," *Cisco Blogs*, May 19, 2020, https://blogs.cisco.com/diversity/the-cisco-customer-experience-journey-to-an-inclusive-culture-leveraging-the-power-of-proximity.

3. Ibid.

4. Emily Crockett, "The Amazing Tool That Women in the White House Used to Fight Gender Bias," *Vox*, September 14, 2016, https://www.vox.com/2016/9/14/12914370/white-house-obama-women-gender-bias-amplification.

5. Lucas Shaw and Bloomberg, "Netflix Will Move $100 Million into Black-Owned Banks," *Fortune*, June 30, 2020, https://fortune.com/2020/06/30/netflix-100-million-black-owned-banks/.

6. Goldman Sachs, "One Million Black Women," accessed May 9, 2021, https://www.goldmansachs.com/our-commitments/sustainability/one-million-black-women/.
7. Adidas (@adidas), "Black Lives Matter," Instagram, June 10, 2020, https://www.instagram.com/p/CBRDCkFgg9R/.

## Chapter 6

1. Josh Bersin, "Elevating Equity and Diversity: The Challenge of the Decade," Josh Bersin, February 11, 2021, https://joshbersin.com/2021/02/elevating-equity-and-diversity-the-challenge-of-the-decade/.
2. Elizabeth Weise, "Google Discloses Its (Lack of) Diversity," *USA TODAY*, May 28, 2014, https://www.usatoday.com/story/tech/2014/05/28/google-releases-employee-diversity-figures/9697049/.
3. Cyrus Taraporevala, "Fearless Girl's Shattered Ceilings: Why Diversity in Leadership Matters," State Street Global Advisors (SSGA), March 8, 2021, https://www.ssga.com/us/en/institutional/ic/insights/fearless-girls-shattered-ceilings-why-diversity-in-leadership.
4. Jon Chesto, "Firm Behind 'Fearless Girl' Statue to Pay $5M over Equal Pay for Women, Minorities," *Boston Globe*, October 5, 2017, https://www.bostonglobe.com/business/2017/10/05/state-street-boston-based-firm-behind-fearless-girl-statue-pay-case-alleging-pay-discrimination-against-women-minorities/ZJoCFfgrUrWDb9bNTdrcRN/story.html.
5. Vivek Kaul, "The Necktie Syndrome: Why CEOs Tend to Be Significantly Taller Than the Average Male," *Economic Times*, September 30, 2011, https://economictimes.indiatimes.com/the-necktie-syndrome-why-ceos-tend-to-be-significantly-taller-than-the-average-male/articleshow/10178115.cms?from=mdr.
6. Arik Hesseldahl, "Salesforce CEO Benioff Takes Stand Against Indiana Anti-gay Law," *Vox*, March 26, 2015, https://www.vox.com/2015/3/26/11560746/salesforce-ceo-benioff-takes-stand-against-indiana-anti-gay-law.
7. Elizabeth Lopato, "To Expose Sexism at Uber, Susan Fowler Blew up Her Life," *Verge*, February 19, 2020, https://www.theverge.com/2020/2/19/21142081/susan-fowler-uber-whistleblower-interview-silicon-valley-discrimination-harassment.
8. *New York Times*, "Uber Report: Eric Holder's Recommendations for Change," June 13, 2017, https://www.nytimes.com/2017/06/13/technology/uber-report-eric-holders-recommendations-for-change.html.
9. Jenny Strasburg, "Abercrombie Recalls T-shirts Many Found Offensive," *SFGate*, April 19, 2002, https://www.sfgate.com/news/article/Abercrombie-recalls-T-shirts-many-found-offensive-2849480.php.
10. Brandee J. Tecson, "Abercrombie Pulls T-shirts After Teen Girls Launch Boycott," *MTV News*, November 7, 2005, http://www.mtv.com/news/1513153/abercrombie-pulls-t-shirts-after-teen-girls-launch-boycott/.

11. Matthew Wilson, "The Rise and Fall—and Rise Again—of Abercrombie & Fitch," *Business Insider*, March 26, 2020, https://www.businessinsider.com/history-of-clothing-brand-abercrombie-and-fitch#its-sales-began-to-fall-in-the-late-2000s-as-public-interest-waned-11.

## Chapter 7

1. Toby Roger, "Diversity and Inclusion Survey: Building a More Inclusive Future," *Culture Amp*, https://www.cultureamp.com/blog/diversity-and-inclusion-survey.
2. Lean In, "Women Are Paid Less Than Men—and That Hits Harder in an Economic Crisis," https://leanin.org/equal-pay-data-about-the-gender-pay-gap.
3. Colorado Department of Labor and Employment, "Equal Pay for Equal Work Act, Part 2," https://cdle.colorado.gov/equalpaytransparency.
4. *World at Work*, "Pay Equity and DE&I 2020: How Are We Doing?," October 28, 2020, https://www.worldatwork.org/press-room/pay-equity-and-de-i-2020-how-are-we-doing.
5. Lean In, "Women Are Paid Less Than Men."
6. Tyler Clifford, "Nielsen CEO Explains Why He Took on the Additional Role of Chief Diversity Officer," CNBC, June 19, 2020, https://www.cnbc.com/2020/06/19/white-nielsen-ceo-explains-decision-to-become-chief-diversity-officer.html.
7. IBM, *Diversity & Inclusion*, June 2015, https://www.ibm.com/employment/inclusion/pdf/ibm_diversity_brochure.pdf.
8. David A. Thomas, "Diversity as Strategy," *Harvard Business Review*, September 2004, https://hbr.org/2004/09/diversity-as-strategy.
9. Human Rights Watch, "Covid-19 Fueling Anti-Asian Racism and Xenophobia Worldwide," May 12, 2020, https://www.hrw.org/news/2020/05/12/covid-19-fueling-anti-asian-racism-and-xenophobia-worldwide#.

## Chapter 8

1. Richard Fry and Kim Parker, "Early Benchmarks Show 'Post-Millennials' on Track to Be Most Diverse, Best-Educated Generation Yet," Pew Research Center, November 15, 2018, https://www.pewresearch.org/social-trends/2018/11/15/early-benchmarks-show-post-millennials-on-track-to-be-most-diverse-best-educated-generation-yet/.
2. Jennifer Miller, "For Younger Job Seekers, Diversity and Inclusion in the Workplace Aren't a Preference. They're a Requirement," *Washington Post*, February 18, 2021, https://www.washingtonpost.com/business/2021/02/18/millennial-genz-workplace-diversity-equity-inclusion/.
3. Sheryl Estrada, "D&I Roles Have More Than Doubled Since 2015, Report Says," *HR Dive*, July 9, 2020, https://www.hrdive.com/news/di-roles-have-more-than-doubled-since-2015-report-says/581309/.

4. Marshall Goldsmith, *What Got You Here Won't Get You There* (New York: Hyperion Books, 2007).

5. Libby Hoffman, "10 Models for Design Thinking," *Medium*, July 29, 2016, https://medium.com/@elizabeth7hoffman/10-models-for-design-thinking-f6943e4ee068.

6. IDEO, "Design Thinking Defined," accessed April 4, 2021, https://design-thinking.ideo.com/.

7. Aaron K. Chatterji and Michael W. Toffel, "The New CEO Activists," *Harvard Business Review*, January-February 2018, https://hbr.org/2018/01/the-new-ceo-activists.

8. Goldman Sachs, "Goldman Sachs' Commitment to Board Diversity," February 4, 2020, https://www.goldmansachs.com/our-commitments/diversity-and-inclusion/launch-with-gs/pages/commitment-to-diversity.html.

9. Cecil Harris, "Major League Baseball's Decision to Move the All-Star Game out of Georgia Was a Grand Slam," *NBC News*, April 5, 2021, https://www.nbcnews.com/think/opinion/major-league-baseball-s-decision-move-all-star-game-out-ncna1263074.

10. David A. Bell, Dawn Bell, and Jennifer J. Hitchcok, "New Law Requires Diversity on Boards of California-Based Companies," Harvard Law School Forum on Corporate Governance, October 10, 2020, https://corpgov.law.harvard.edu/2020/10/10/new-law-requires-diversity-on-boards-of-california-based-companies/.

11. Ron S. Berenblat, Elizabeth Gonzalez-Sussman, and Olshan Frome Wolosky, "Nasdaq Proposes New Listing Rules Related to Board Diversity," Harvard Law School Forum on Corporate Governance, December 13, 2020, https://corpgov.law.harvard.edu/2020/12/13/nasdaq-proposes-new-listing-rules-related-to-board-diversity/.

12. U.S. House of Representatives Committee on Financial Services, *Diversity and Inclusion: Holding America's Large Banks Accountable*, February 2020, https://docs.house.gov/meetings/BA/BA13/20200212/110498/HHRG-116-BA13-20200212-SD003-U1.pdf.

13. Cyrus Taraporevala, "Fearless Girl's Shattered Ceilings: Why Diversity in Leadership Matters," State Street Global Advisors (SSGA), March 8, 2021, https://www.ssga.com/us/en/institutional/ic/insights/fearless-girls-shattered-ceilings-why-diversity-in-leadership.

14. Saijel Kishan, "BlackRock to Push Companies on Racial Diversity in 2021," *Bloomberg Equality*, December 9, 2020, https://www.bloomberg.com/news/articles/2020-12-10/blackrock-plans-to-push-companies-on-racial-diversity-in-2021.

15. Matteo Tonello, "2021 Proxy Season Preview and Shareholder Voting Trends (2017–2020)," Harvard Law School Forum on Corporate Governance, February 11, 2021, https://corpgov.law.harvard.edu/2021/02/11/2021-proxy-season-preview-and-shareholder-voting-trends-2017-2020/.

16. Kathy Gurchiek, "Employee Activism Is on the Rise," SHRM, September 12, 2019, https://www.shrm.org/hr-today/news/hr-news/pages/employee-activism-on-the-rise.aspx.

17. Daisuke Wakabayashi, "Google Ends Forced Arbitration for All Employee Disputes," *New York Times*, February 21, 2019, https://www.nytimes.com/2019/02/21/technology/google-forced-arbitration.html.

18. Jeff Beer, "One Year Later, What Did We Learn from Nike's Blockbuster Colin Kaepernick Ad?," *Fast Company*, September 5, 2019, https://www.fastcompany.com/90399316/one-year-later-what-did-we-learn-from-nikes-block-buster-colin-kaepernick-ad.

19. Kim-Mai Cutler, "How Lever Got To 50-50 Women and Men," Medium, January 13, 2017, https://medium.com/initialized-capital/how-lever-got-to-50-50-between-women-men-b8db05b7d3ee.

# Index

# About the Author

**Cynthia Owyoung** is VP of Inclusion, Equity, and Belonging at Robinhood, where she drives the company's approach to enhancing its culture of diversity and inclusion. As the founder of Breaking Glass Forums, she develops strategies to accelerate an increase in more diverse leaders and inclusive organizations.

She has established and led diversity and inclusion initiatives for 20 years at organizations both large and small, including Charles Schwab, GitHub, Yahoo!, and Intuit. Cynthia is known for integrating a diversity and inclusion lens into all aspects of the business, from talent management to product development. She has been recognized among *Entrepreneur* magazine's 100 Women of Impact in 2021, Canvas's Top 100+ Remarkable Women in HR in 2021, North America's Most Influential D&I Leaders in 2020 by Hive Learning, and the Global Diversity List 2020.

Cynthia has been a featured speaker at conferences and events hosted by TEDx, Women in Tech International, Tech Inclusion, the Anita Borg Institute, the Conference Board, and USC's Center for Effective Organizations, among others. She has been interviewed in multiple outlets, including the *Huffington Post*, LinkedIn's *Talent Blog*, and *Diversity Woman Magazine*.

Prior to her calling in human resources, Cynthia launched a strategic planning consultancy, increasing the capabilities of nonprofit and for-profit organizations in organizational development, brand marketing, and business strategy. She also built a decade-long career as a brand strategist for leading global companies and advertising agencies, developing campaigns for Microsoft, Levi Strauss, and Apple.

Cynthia currently serves on the board of directors for AbilityPath, a nonprofit dedicated to empowering people with special needs to achieve their full potential. She has served on the steering committee of the Silicon Valley Chief Diversity Officers Consortium, launched the Bay Area Diversity Peer Network, and chaired the Employee Resource Group Advisory Council.

She earned an MBA in human resources from UCLA's Anderson School of Management and two bachelor's degrees, one in marketing and finance from UC Berkeley's Haas Business School and another in psychology, also from UC Berkeley.

For more information, please visit www.breaking.glass.